THE ACCIDENTAL WRITING LAB

THE ACCIDENTAL WRITING LAB

Jane,
Write your
Sunday Brunch ideas!
There are people who
need the love and
the laughter.
Sheila M Sullivan

SHEILA M. SULLIVAN

The Accidental Writing Lab is non-fiction. Names of children have been changed. Names of most others have been changed except where express consent was given for me to use the real name.

I have a special call out to my editor, Kristen Tate, who worked with me to keep the roughness of the original writing.

All errors, issues, and things that cause the writing to be less than perfect are there on purpose. Not really, it means they slipped through for one reason or the other and keep this work real. *The Accidental Writing Lab* does contain errors. These were kept in to show the good, the bad, and the ugly. Not to mention keeping the integrity of the pieces as they were written. To show you that you can tell a story without perfect grammar. The spelling has been run through the editors. I really hate misspelling words. Yes. This is the author speaking right now. Relax over the mistakes in this novel and go make your own.

You can reach me through my website, www.sheilamsullivan.com or drop me a note at info@sheilamsullivan.com

ISBN 978-0-9989648-3-6

Book Layout and Cover Design by Phillip Gessert www.gessertbooks.com

TABLE OF CONTENTS

BRING ON THE WORDS

I am a writer. Specifically, I write stories and some of these stories have been published as books. "How did I know I wanted to write stories?" That's a great question and my answer, like my writing, continues to evolve. Unlike those who claim they are organized people, I can't tell you that I knew I wanted to write before I was born. Or that I was born to be a writer and I came out of the womb with pen and paper, writing with proper spelling and using complete sentences, resulting in perfect prose. My life has never been that ordered, and I was often told by teachers that maybe I need to focus on something other than writing. That comment came from more than one writing instructor who did not appreciate my ability to write in fragments.

I think back to these bumps along my writing road and realize I did not conform; some teachers interpreted a lack of following instructions as a lack of talent. I saw it as creative intelligence. More often their criticism was not based on my tortured misuse of grammar, but on the content of my writing. Like the time I wrote a paper in my world religions class about how the Catholic church fit all the criteria for being classified a cult. That paper did not receive a passing grade from the teacher, who happened to be more Catholic than the Pope. Once out in this world, I never called myself a writer but I dreamed about it. I flailed and flopped about, sometimes hitting a target or goal, but mostly breaking windows and light fixtures.

My accidental writing lab, which I am giving you a good tour through in this book, was another form of flailing and flopping. How does one write by accident? You ask such great questions. The writing wasn't accidental, but the collection was. The pieces in this book were meant to be short, humorous writing exercises that would prime me for the *real* writing I was trying to do, on my first novel. I emailed them to friends, but I didn't write them intending to collect them in a formal way. I did not completely understand what sort of writing alchemy I had created with these pieces until after the completion of the first two novels, *Spectrum* and *Illumination*, in my F.O.K. series.

What's it like writing a novel? Well, for me, writing a novel is often a hidden and solitary experience. You, our audience, the readers, rarely get to see behind the scenes into the sometimes crazy, chaotic, and inspired sausage-making of a novel. (Note: No pigs or other animals were harmed in the writing of my books.) Like you, I am a reader and while I write, I do consider my reading audience. There are some writers who claim they never consider their readers. My own philosophy on considering the reader is that I want my stories to be read. I appreciate those who take their time to read something I have created, and I am honored when they care enough to share their ideas and opinions—good or bad—about my stories.

Now that I'm no longer worried about failing out of school, writing is such a pleasure. It's not always easy though. Where did the motivation come from to slog through what amounted to thousands of hours over years of writing? Why write? Are you seriously going to eat that piece of paper? You do realize it is not actually sausage? Those are some of the questions you might be contemplating as you read through my account of my writing life.

I was born. *Obviously*, you are thinking, and I know some eyes are rolling back. This will be short and provide some context to my writing voice. Sometimes I do feel that I had 'question authority' written into my DNA chain where others had organization and the ability to spell correctly written into theirs. Hence the paper challenging a high school world religions class. Before that fun, I went to kindergartens. Yes, you read the plural of that word. (Note to my editor…it needs to be left as a plural and this is not creative spelling.) In this lifetime, I went to more than one kindergarten. Call me lucky because I spent some awesome years in the best grade ever created. If you are going to repeat a grade, this is the one I would suggest. My kindergarten tour started in Minnesota. My parents, following the trend of the early seventies, put me in a very well-regarded Montessori school in Minneapolis.

What I discovered in that highly touted Montessori school was painting. After three months of me doing nothing but painting, my career as a painter was derailed. In a sense, I was demoted from the major league in Montessori kindergarten and sent down to a minor league preschool. In preschool I learned that some kids eat the dried macaroni and lick glue. I painted. After my tour in the major and minor league schools in Minnesota, my parents booked me back into the major leagues in a kindergarten in Medina, which is located on the beautiful shores of Lake Washington.

Now, my main manager and booking agent, Mom, claimed I really did not repeat kindergarten per se. Her story was that my birthdate made me a kindergarten pro—something about being born at the end of October preventing me from starting kindergarten. That gives me pause as I wonder about the 'you only painted' comment. Maybe the tour of kindergartens across the states was more about the alphabet. I spent more years in a combination of preschool and kindergarten than most kids.

It wasn't all bad, this multistate tour of kindergartens. I finally advanced past kindergarten in Eureka, California. If you lost count, that makes four kindergartens. Some advantages of this: I was the first sixth grader to get a driver's license; I was easily spotted in the class photos as I was the tallest kid for several years; and I got all those extra years of books being read to me. The teachers were great, but they could not hold a candle to our mother who read to us at home.

I felt so special as she read to us books that she loved as a young girl, passing her love of literature on to us. We had a huge overstuffed brown reclining chair in the living room. Usually my younger sister and I would pile into the chair and Mom would read us these most amazing stories. Those hours spent when we were young listening to her read us such epics as *The Wind in the Willows, The Lion, the Witch and the Wardrobe, The Secret Garden, Winnie-the-Pooh, The Five Little Peppers and How They Grew,* remain some of my fondest memories. The list of books Mom read to us would fill its own volume.

What does all this have to do with this book and the accidental writing lab? Well, to clear something up—I didn't get my driver's license in sixth grade. That was a joke. In all seriousness, my path to writing was as crazy fun as my three-state kindergarten tour. I do believe this helped establish my powers of observation and my philosophy that nap time is still very important, especially in the writing process. I do support taking daily naps and highly recommend them.

Another observation from childhood comes from the gifting of books. Whenever our parents traveled, they would return home with a new book for each one of us. Mom had us read through the Newbery Award winners. Dad's choices were often historical, hard science, or science fiction. Dad introduced me to Douglas Adams when I was twelve. We shared love and laughter over his stories. When my father spent his last five weeks of life with us, he requested I read a couple of his favorite passages from *The Hitchhiker's Guide to the Galaxy*. Dad heard his last story in early November 2016.

Both parents supported and cultivated the family's love for books. The realization that I could create a book came to me at age four. My mom had written and illustrated a book for me titled *The Snow and the Bunny*. That special book is in my office as I write now. She hand-painted the beautiful pictures and told the story of my sister and I and the bunnies in our yard in Eden Prairie, Minnesota—the place where my kindergarten tour started.

I do remember my first attempt at writing, illustrating, and publishing my own children's book forty-five or so years ago. That first book was heavy on the pictures. I loved writing in crayon pictures. This first book was a non-fiction propaganda piece; I tried to use it to convince my parents that Suzie, a beautiful and most loved strawberry roan Shetland pony, needed to live with me in my room. That first foray into the power of story did not result in a pony being my roommate. Instead, I had the pleasure of sharing a room with my younger sister. However, I do believe my sister might have enjoyed having the pony as a roommate too.

I would not write or illustrate another book for forty plus years after that first edition one copy in print. Not exactly sure why I stopped supporting the dream of writing and creating books. What this meant was that I followed a more traditional route. I went to college after finally advancing out of kindergarten and all those grades in between K and college. After working for a while, I looked around and thought that stand-up comedy was a great choice. From stand-up comedy, I went to law school. The irony is not lost on me. I went to law school because the tools of the lawyers' trade were books and words.

I thought it would be fun, and the comedy clubs were closing left and right. It quickly became apparent that most lawyers are not funny, and they drink and smoke more than the comedians do. I am allergic to smoke. I have since recalibrated my concept of fun.

I entered the practice of law and had turned my crayons in for a laptop. Do not be sad, I bought some more crayons and do use them. The law allowed me to write daily and to use books. Research became one of my strong suits. It was a good fit for a while. My serious addiction to reading served me well. I was paid to read. That was brilliant. What I failed to do was connect my own internal dots—those breadcrumbs of plot ideas, funny happenings, and stories that would populate my mind. I would brush them away with my broom of responsibility to focus on my *real* job. It did not matter that I wanted to share stories that helped people laugh, relate, and walk away with something good. Law was not a career of happy. Most of the legal writing I read left me banging my head against the top of my desk. It was horrid. The writing was mired in language paradigms meant to obscure and confuse. This was not writing that brought laughter or warm feelings. Well, sometimes the writing brought laughter because, while I might be a writer of fragments, lawyers are the writers of the longest sentences ever. I read a brief from opposing counsel that had one sentence span two and half pages. Crazy!

Throughout the years spent in the legal realm, the characters and voices in my head kept developing and they were challenging me to write their stories. They finally grew so intense I could no longer ignore them. This makes it sound like I am suffering from a personality disorder. Nope. I appreciate my own quick denial on being on a personality disorder spectrum. But what happened next was that the stories of these characters started flowing. Sometimes on a piece of paper during a meeting. Other times while waiting in an airport. Bits and pieces started to knit themselves into more than a random scene or idea—they were stories. I would quickly hide these stories and my characters in my thinly veiled attempts to return to the law.

I'm not sure now sure who I hid them from? Most likely myself. I knew my desire was to write a novel. I may have mentioned such a lofty goal to others in passing. For the most part, I was a closeted writer. It is so much easier to write in a dark closet with a laptop that has a lit keyboard than admit that I had characters talking to me. I would work all day at the office or be in court and then come home and write. People would ask what I was doing with my life, and I would fall back on the fading shadows of my law practice. That always led them to ask me what kind of lawyer I was. The characters in my head waiting to have their stories recorded would try to put words in my mouth. "You're a writer, not a lawyer." I would shove those voices down and fit my answer to the person inquiring. You ask why I hid? Why all this drama?

My answer is this: I was following a path that others approved of and supported. The writing was not supported (most by my self-talk) and thought to be a wrong turn. One excuse I often cite is approval; also, I enjoyed when I actually was able to help others through the law. Not to mention the money aspects of a law practice were quite nice. The actual reality as to the slow, oh-so-slow transition into writing was that I was a big mess of procrastination wrapped in a blanket of fear.

I waited for motivation to bless me, and I waited by watching countless hours of television, wandering through the aisles of bookstores, and talking with anyone who would chat. My wife, Janine, continues to this day in her unwavering support of my writing. She never demanded to see what I had written. She is so sweet and genuinely curious about the words pouring out of me into the computer. Janine would witness my mad crazy typing, scribbling ideas on whatever would take ink, and moments when my body was in the room but clearly my mind was elsewhere creating plot lines, characters, and epic stories. She might share with you her frustrations of talking to me only to have me transfixed like a teenager playing a video game.

When I felt some confidence in my writing, I would share my work with Janine. She is my safe harbor. If she were talking with you right now, she would point out that I was my most chatty about plots, characters, and stories after midnight. In my defense, it was only after I asked her if she was awake. She would mumble something and that was my ticket to talk or in some cases fire up the laptop and read aloud to her my latest creation.

To read aloud what one has written is the fastest way to learn if the writing flows or not. The difficulty in reading aloud is in trying to gage the reaction of the person forced to listen. I spent much of my time in a state of anxious hand wringing, and if I bit my nails I would have done that too. That makes reading aloud rather difficult. Don't bite your nails and attempt to read aloud. It annoys those attempting to listen. I would search for any signs of her reactions to my prose. Did she like it? Of course, she would say she thinks what I write is brilliant, she's married to me. There might be an underlying agenda here since she hopes that, once done with a writing project, I will help with the house work. If you followed my writing you might know that I use writing to procrastinate about doing laundry, among other chores. With all this procrastination you might wonder how I get anything done. I am pondering that and will get back to you with an answer.

How did I finally let go of the law to write? To answer this question, I must turn to the freedom Janine brought to my life. This now becomes a love story. Cue the romantic candlelight, chocolate, and fine wine. I had fallen in love with another attorney. Relax. The other attorney is my wife, Janine. She is the exception that proves my rule about lawyers: she is funny, does not smoke and only uses her legal brain to do good. One way she does good with her legal mind is by expanding her vision of work. Not limited by brick and mortar legal work, she combined her law with her engineering background and jumped into the business world. She is similar to a hotshot fire jumper. Janine parachutes into business programs on fire and helps those teams find their critical paths through the chaos, putting out fires and restoring function to the teams. What I did not anticipate in this was that I would be on the plane with her and jumping into the unknown too. My characters, in tow, jumped with us. All these changes helped me grow up and grab ahold of my passion to write.

People, as in friends, have asked why we live like nomads. Here is the short answer. When we first met, Janine had been all set to move Australia. She had a life established there. I upended that life for her and she, in return, changed my concept of a traditional life. Had I not joined her on the road, I might not have found my writing voice. Our time together has found us moving so often that we have been questioned by close family and friends about our status in a witness protection program. I can confirm that we are not part of one or in need of one. Yet.

My road out of the writer's closet happened in fits and spurts thanks to this unconventional life with Janine. There were many moments when I questioned myself about stepping off the cliff away from practicing law. As we moved from city to city, I was given more and more material to pull into my writing. Sometimes we are in a city for a few months to a year or two. This type of roaming is not exactly ideal for establishing a law practice.

As the years piled up and I moved further from the brick and mortar law office, I became more comfortable sharing that I am a writer. The closet door cracked open. With each book that is written and published, I am further from that closet and out in the sun. It feels amazing. What I learned is that most people I talked with out in this big wide world were either writing a book or felt they should be writing a book. They were all so eager to share. Then when they learned that I have two books out in the world, the questions on how to do it followed. How to write a book, that is—not the "it" as defined by one of our past presidents.

When we were living in San Quentin Village, California, I finally flung the door open, exposing myself as a writer. I was at the start of herding multiple ideas into my first book. You are curious about San Quentin? I was not living in the prison. I would like to point out that San Quentin State Prison is a penitentiary for men only. No, we did not have a mug shots, orange uniforms, or jail cell numbers. I appreciate that many of you believe all lawyers belong in prison.

During the San Quentin Village foray, I attended my first writer's conference, sponsored by Book Passage, a wonderful book store that hosts some great workshops. It was a mystery writer's conference. The authors and writers I met at that event that long-ago July were inspiring, interesting, and downright scary. I sat in discussions where they were talking about different creative ways to kill people. These otherwise soft-spoken, intelligent, and kind humans were coming up with ideas that kept me awake and unable to sleep. Was I a mystery writer? I came back on the second day and posed that question to one of the guest speakers over a cup of coffee.

I shared with him that maybe I wanted to write comedy and romance. His response has stayed with me. He warned me to stay away from the romance writers because they create these fantastical romantic stories and there is no way any real human could ever live up to it. Thus, they tend to be an angry, grumpy lot. Stick with mystery writers, he advised, because here we get to live out our aggressions on the page and are therefore are a whole lot more fun in life. (He also told me to attend Amy Stewart's talk on poisonous plants, and I can tell you that this, at least, was very good advice. I have her books and highly recommend them for mystery writers and criminal defense lawyers.)

Another result of that writer's conference that seems counter to the inspiration was the self-talk wanting me to run back into the closet and quit. Creative brain that I have, I worked myself into self-inflicted defeat after reading one of my stories to a small group in a breakout session at the writer's workshop. Unlike the other writers' pieces, mine was devoid of bloody murder scenes and a detective. Instead, I had a minister of soul collection and he took a baby's soul. When I had finished reading my story to the group, I was met with silence. No one said a word. When others had read their stories, they were met with lots of comments and suggestions. Silence. This took me back to doing stand-up and staring out at a silent audience. Was I crazy? Why did I think I could be a writer? A couple people shifted in their chairs, uncomfortable with the silence.

That silence felt like it was an hour long. We are talking deathly *silence,* people. Then a wonderful and amazing thing happened. One of my literary idols, who was in our small group, spoke up. She shared that the story was the most disturbing thing she had heard and created quite the image in her head. I will never forget her saying, "It takes courage to kill a baby in the first two pages of your story. It makes me want to read more." Still shell-shocked from the silence, I took her words as encouraging.

Why is that amazing? I received emotional feedback from a woman who is a writer and published author with millions of books sold. She later encouraged me to finish that story. I am still working on that one and hope to have it out soon. Some other characters elbowed their way in, and I have written their stories first. It might be because "disturbing" was not the emotion I was going for and really wanted the other end of the emotional spectrum like "laughter."

The writer's conference concluded, and I had received some interest in that story from a couple literary agents. Those follow-ups died. Discouraged from the lack of continued interest, I focused on Janine and I getting packed up for our next move. I also procrastinated on my writing with a list of about a hundred books to read on writing. I read them. Reading will always be in my comfort zone—the need to study the craft of writing when not actually writing down your stories. When we moved from the San Francisco Bay area to Dallas, Texas, I was terrified.

I was not terrified of Texas. Well, I was slightly terrified of moving from a blue state to a red state. But I fell in love with the folks we met in Dallas. I did not fall in love with the weather that produced heat hotter than an oven and hail storms that could break your head open. By this point, I had declared that I was writing full time. I continued my procrastination in my declared career and read those books on writing, publishing, and grammar. My editor might raise her eyebrows over that last admission. I really did read books on grammar. No. I have not read any books on spelling.

These writing days or not writing days were prior to my discovery of Ponder Points, the little stories that turned into my accidental writing lab. I still had some magical thinking that the Grand Dame, Saint Motivation herself, would bless me with perfect sentences and prose. I did have days where I had some heavy word counts. I would type out page after page of a story that had no direction. Well, actually, it had several directions. Each one of the characters had their point of view expressed. Trust me, this is not the way to write. My attempts to control the characters and formalize a plot made the writing appear forced and nothing close to professional. As I shared earlier, this wild writing over the days, weeks, months would be peppered with my trips, more like pilgrimages, to the bookstores of Dallas wondering how published authors pulled it off. How did those writers get their ideas out of their heads, printed, and published? I was most curious about how they restricted the point of view to one character or sometimes two. Not to mention the fact that I, as the reader, did not see the days, weeks, years taken to write and rewrite those stories. No. In my world, it looked like those writers had perfect grammar and spelling from the start to finish of their books. It was all instant and perfect. Then I remembered a quote I stumbled across by Joyce Carol Oates: "The first sentence can't be written until the final sentence is written."

Sit down and write. That became my mantra. This did not stop all the questions in my head. Why did it take so long? This was my job? Where were my words? Where was the story? I am a writer. Am I a professional writer? What determines professional? What about success? My advice to anyone in the creative arts: get your work captured in your medium. That is the first success. My medium is words and sometimes crayon pictures. I manage the cart and work at keeping it behind the horse. Right now, as I am constantly learning this writing craft, I deal with a whole lot of writing that stinks worse than manure. Proof that I am walking behind the horse.

When you are in the thick of your day-in-day-out living, it might be hard to see your success as you capture your creative output. My writing world changes daily. This freedom also brings a wealth of experiences clamoring to be captured. The birth of Ponder Points happened because of this freedom and by the courage to follow the happy accidents that happen in life. I would have my computer open and be typing away when something or someone would jump into the flow. At first, I was frustrated and blamed the paused writing and frustrations on the chaos of not having any one place to work. There was no room of my own. Granted, I did have a hotel room and it was always clean and the towels refreshed. In each new location, I had the yearning and the curiosity to get out and explore. It was these intrusions into my concentration that landed the accidental writing lab in my lap.

The exploration and numerous coffee houses helped me learn how to focus. In putting one word after another, I began to find a balance in writing and living. This writing allowed me to access the writing muscle in my brain without the stress of writing a full-length novel. Ponder Points were situations that actually happened, and they challenged me to write without my internal critic. To tell the story and nothing more. Most of these situations caused me to laugh. When I wrote these happenings down, it created my bridge into my writer brain. This became my motivation key, although I wasn't truly aware of that fact until I collected all these Points together. Welcome to my accidental writing lab.

I learned that my motivation to write renews itself from within daily through the actions I take as a writer. Motivation does not find me. I create it. It took me a while to realize this particular aspect of my writing life. Maybe because of Hollywood and self-created romantic concepts of the writing life, I believed the twin sirens, Motivation and Inspiration, would come looking for me. They would announce themselves with trumpets and sparkles. Time would melt away and every sentence I typed would be eloquent perfection. That was the dream.

Here is the reality: *The Accidental Writing Lab* and Ponder Points came into my brain and opened my internal motivation and passion. I do love writing. I see your skeptical head-shaking because you have read a couple hundred words of me doing everything but writing. You ask, why write? When you go on about procrastination, fear, and lack of motivation? If I do not write, my brain, my life is out of sorts. To write brings order to my chaos and views in life. I do write fiction. The world of my fiction comes from the life around me. It filters through my levels of self-observation and reflections.

Another reason I write comes from fear. Fear can be an amazing energy resource. This is not the fear of being good at writing. Well, that is part of the fear. Yes, I want to write well. This fear has to do with the stories and characters I meet through reading and my own writing. Edgar Allen Poe, Stephen King, P.D. James, Tana French, Louise Penny, and many others who write stories that scare me so much I sleep with a light on at night. Sometimes I wonder how I could create a character that goes on a killing spree? Or a story line that leaves people speechless due to the horror it paints in their own imaginations. It is diving into those fears of our human experience that also propels me to write.

My first book had many very scary thriller scenes. I understand after looking at the cutting of hundreds of pages and scenes that at heart I am a mystery writer. I stumbled at first and took out most of that in my first book and the F.O.K. series. This inner conflict is also what motivated me to rewrite a story, creating more than eighty drafts. My drafts had grown to more than eight hundred pages, give or take a hundred. In Dallas, I happened to be in a Barnes & Noble coffee shop and I had a bad day. My computer screen was acting as a blank reflection of my mind. My characters were quiet. I had nothing. Silence. My brain was quiet—almost peaceful. Was that it? Had I written my last words? What would I tell Janine? Would I have to give up? No. I do not want to go back to practicing law. Been there, done that, and decided I like people too much to be a lawyer. Then, in the midst of this bad day, the most wonderful thing happened. Life.

That day as I sat wondering if a second cup of coffee and a cinnamon roll would help spur my writing, a rather animated conversation between two soccer moms caught my attention. In an instant, something clicked inside, and I switched off my internal editor at my mainframe, located somewhere deep in my brain, and gave myself five minutes to record what I was witnessing. That first observational writing captured the discussion between these two moms on the importance of using Febreze to get the smell of teenage boys out of their house. I do not include that first writing in this collection because it was on a computer that crashed and I had not backed it up. This is a service announcement for your own sanity. I implore you to back up your work. Go do it now, I'll wait. Back to that first writing: I did not think anything of the exercise other than I filled two pages on an open Word document.

The exercise opened up something in my brain, and I went from the five-minute writing exercise into my novel. Words poured out, and the characters came alive, jostling for position. At this point, I did not know that this was my key to writing; I actually thought it was a one-time thing. When we moved from Dallas to Fargo, I shared the writing exercise concept with Janine. Fargo gave me more material and situations to capture. I shared these with Janine. She suggested I share them with some of our friends. The emails went out and the responses gave me positive and insightful feedback on my writing.

I affectionately titled my writing exercises Ponder Points. During the writing and rewriting of *Spectrum*, I wrote over a hundred Ponder Points—on some days, they were the only words written. These wonderful short snippets of sometimes crazy life happenings were what built my motivation and inspiration for writing one word at a time. With two books published and a third in the works, I was ready to write. Life had a different plan. I joined the flu and pneumonia train in January 2018, when I had planned on writing book three in the F.O.K. series. I was too sick to read and definitely could not write. As

I won the battle and started to feel better, the Ponder Points collection gave me another entry into writing.

It was that day in March when I realized through the laughter that I had created my own writing lab. This is not new. I am not the first writer to do this, and I will not be the last. My Ponder Points were unconditional writing exercises where I gave myself the freedom to tell a story, record a scene, and report through words about life. And in that reporting, I would pick an idea in the craft of writing to work into the scene. No judgments.

Ponder Points also helped me in the shaping of my first book and the F.O.K. series. I wanted to infuse the laughter I captured in the Ponder Points into the novel. With *Spectrum* I made a choice to edit out many of the darker scenes as the story developed more through Frances, the protagonist, and she is not a murdering type, nor is she a detective. (I spent a lot of time talking to medical examiners, police officers, and doctors about topics like how people kill and what an autopsy can and cannot tell you. When doing this type of research, it is very important to stress that you are writing a fiction novel and this is research for your scary characters.) Some of those scenes cut from *Spectrum* might be used in the murder/thriller novel. That reminds me to tell you: if you are a writer, keep your edits, your pieces of scribble, and brief notes. You never know when you will use them. Maybe never and maybe sooner than you think.

Back to the first book. How, then, was it so difficult to sit down and write the story? To get that first book done? I dealt with the self-talk megaphone telling me that I was not ready to publish. The story still needed to be tweaked. At this point I also learned that it was okay to be flexible as I wrote a comedy/drama/murder/thriller/coming-out story. Life is confusing and so is writing.

Part of the issue for conception and writing was resolved when I stopped my inner editor/critic. Ponder Points did help with my writing flow as it helped quiet my internal editor. That self-talking overly confident inner editor was not a friend. I read some books on how to silence that inner critic, and I listened to other writers' stories about conquering their own demons. All of the advice boiled down to this: put your butt down in a chair and get the words out. That's the essence of being a writer. So, I wrote.

This makes it sound like I was on the road to easy street. But that's not exactly the truth as my creative writing started in spurts—a lot like when I first learned how to drive my VW Dasher diesel stick shift on the hills of San Francisco. You might believe you know how to drive a stick shift until you are a new driver on a hill so steep you look out over the hood of the car and only see sky, and you peer in your rearview mirror and see a BMW an inch from your back bumper. There is no room to let your car roll backwards. Add to that the fear that your parents would not appreciate that you drove yourself and three other friends from Eureka, California down to San Francisco on a Saturday without permission. Another story for another time: back to writing motivation, inspiration, and the why I write and why I share this with you.

These short writing exercises became a way for me to share laughter with friends we had made along the way of our travels. It appeared that people enjoyed reading my short musings. They liked opening their emails and spitting coffee, juice, or wine all over their keyboards as spontaneous uncontrolled laughter resulted from reading my accounts. Now, I would like to say that happened every time. It did not. When it did, I heard about it.

The writing exercise took on a dual role as they chronicled our nomadic lifestyle as Janine and I traveled for work, vacation, and fun, all the while trying on different locations as possible home ports for us. We are still searching, learning, and living in different cities searching for our home port.

When we moved from Dallas to Fargo, we carried with us in spirit the wonderful friends made at our latest interlude. What happened was not expected. Our friends started sharing how they loved the short stories and passed them along to their friends. Some added their own understanding of something I had done that was silly or just plain wrong. Sympathy was sent to Janine for having survived something that I had done. After urging from these most supportive friends, I present these Ponder Points and some observations about my non-linear writing process.

I adore laughter that helps us all feel better. This love of laughing can be linked to the Irish side of my life. My dad had this wonderful infectious laugh that could inspire the most gray, dour group to crack a smile and laugh. The situations I focused on for these writing exercises are funny because they are real. I have peculiar math and directional skills. I am blessed with an insatiable and friendly curiosity. Thank god, I am not a cat because I would still be exploring an empty bag somewhere. In some of these accounts one might assume I do not particularly care for children. That is not the case. I am actually quite 'clucky', as Janine says. I adore children and sometimes wish they were minding the government right now.

Now that I think about children—if offered, would I have traded my first-born to be an author? No need to worry. No kids were sacrificed in the writing of *Spectrum*. I do not have any kids and that might be a story for another time. If you're awake when reading these lines, you might think I don't have a kid because I did offer up my child in exchange for the publication of my book. Nope. For those of you who do write and have children, I am in awe of your abilities and powers to do that and am standing at my computer clapping. I do not care what other people think. You get a standing ovation and a huge "Bravo."

Over the course of writing these Ponder Points, most of them funny, all of them written from the heart, through the encouragement of my Ponder Point groupies and my wife, I collected them here for you. The next decision was about how many to include. After pondering this, I came up with a baker's dozen plus more for this first volume. This choice dates me because it is rare to find a bakery that still does a baker's dozen or even knows what that means. In the old days, before 1990-something, a baker would include twelve in a dozen plus one to make thirteen. Many believe that thirteen is an unlucky number. I disagree. For those who are superstitious, I am doing a baker's dozen plus more. Does that mean you will read 14 or 17 Ponder Points? Good question.

The length of most of the Ponder Points really was dictated by how quickly I could capture my thoughts in about five minutes. I believe they are a good length to be enjoyed during a commute, the commode, a coffee break, or to relax with a good laugh before sleeping. When you read one you have accomplished reading something that does have a beginning, middle, and end in a very compact set of words.

This is not a self-help book. I share some insights into the writing of my first novel and that is more a casual conversation than a book on writing. You might find your own inspiration through attempting your own accidental writing lab. If not, maybe the laughter will help. If I have helped you procrastinate, do not give my name to your loved ones waiting for your book to be finished. Although, if you laugh it might help. That said, not all the Ponder Points are funny, for those who sit there with crossed arms daring these words to elicit laughter. Whatever. I consider it a win because you are reading these words. Although I'm not exactly sure how you are reading this book if your arms are crossed.

I do have my own favorite Ponder Points. For those who want to know which ones, I will share that *Glazed Toddler*, *The Tao of Poo*, and *More from the Car Lounge* are at the top of my list. It is my hope that you find your own favorites. They jump out and you find yourself retelling them to someone else as you laugh out loud. Ponder Points exist all around us, and I know I am not the only one to observe the humor in our everyday interactions.

Before I turn you loose into a baker's dozen plus more, I must clear up one more thing. I have been questioned about the numbering system of the Ponder Points. It really is a mystery. I might have been influenced by the numbering system in a small town in the North Bay. There was a block of homes next to a prison where the inhabitants were allowed to pick their own house numbers. Or so the myth has been handed down. That was why we lived in a house that had the number 42. Yes. The same number that the late Douglas Adams wrote as the answer to life, the universe, and everything. I am not making that up. It is where I finally landed on my purpose, to write. Our address was 42 Main Street. The house next to us might have been 1234, the one on the other side was 36. Across the streets were numbers 1, 64, and 89. I'm not sure how the mail was delivered but it was, and I have even more respect for the Postal Workers. Pizza delivery in this area was a whole different issue. Sometimes it was convenient if I had not had dinner plans and a pizza magically showed up. We always paid for it. That happened twice! I have lost count of how many Ponder Points I have written. This collection is not in numerical order, so let it go. You do not need to read them in any order; they stand alone.

Some question the number of times we have moved across this country. How does this relate to the writing of Ponder Points? I found myself writing in some unusual places: Have laptop, will write. The gift that I was given came through the traveling. Along with the excitement of constant change through the travel came the desire to find some sort of continuity, and focus. In the fourteen years we have been together, Janine and I have moved more than twenty times.

As I type these words, I realize that we are getting ready to move again and who knows which way the wind will blow, sending us off to our next adventure.

It is my hope that you read these Ponder Points and enjoy. Be carried away in laughter and in thought. You might be inspired to write. What this is not: It is not a book specifically on writing. There are no hard and fast rules per se. This is what my experience was in opening myself to a career as a writer. These pages contain small snapshots of what I was thinking along the very long road to the publication of my first novel. I share these moments along my journey with you as a way to hopefully inspire you to be messy, let go, and find your own way to write and create. Some might be so organized they use a spreadsheet and plot out every pivot and turn in the story line. Others might dive into the middle of the story and write out to the beginning and the end at the same time. It does not matter as long as you do what works for you. It comes down to the actions or habits that help you create your stories. This is how I work.

Welcome to a glimpse into my accidental writing lab. Enjoy.

PONDER POINTS

What follows are a collection of writing exercises combined with some thoughts about writing as a craft. The Ponder Points are all real. These situations, people, and places were part of our lives. Some names have been changed to protect the innocent; other names have not been changed. The name(s) of all children have been changed, except for the ones related to me. Sorry, nephews. My name and Janine's are real. Janine was most gracious in letting me share our stories without changing her name or mine. She has been and continues to be my most supportive and loving wife in this life.

I have added notes before and after some of the Ponder Points. These notes provide insights into what I was thinking as a writer and where I was in the writing of my first two novels, *Spectrum* and *Illumination.*

One concept that I played with in all of these short stories was where to start the story. At what point do I capture the story to give the reader the perspective I, as the writer, wanted to share. That arbitrary five-minute rule I gave myself helped me find that starting point. It surprised me when I realized the time limit helped. I would quickly walk back through the happenings and then forward to find that point where the story would start—the place that gave it the ground or foundation to help with the humor.

The art of telling a story no matter the length can be learned. In my life I had some great storytellers show me the way. From my Sullivan Irish roots, I learned the art of telling a story. Sometimes, I wonder why it took me so long to let the storyteller out. I knew it was a family legacy with the antics of my Grandpa Carlos and then my dad. Through the years, they treated us to countless stories, some real and some not, but all told with a sincerity and love that would capture anyone who listened.

I knew that I had that ability too. A stint as a stand-up comedian in Seattle gave the storyteller in me an audience. Sometimes there were actual people in the audience. This insight into the art of telling a story came into my writing. It helped me in the construction of the Ponder Points and taught me how much to fill out the story. The mid-point had to hold your attention, give information, and build to the punch line. It was this concept of capturing the punch line that produced the laughter that had me thinking about those times I spent writing jokes for the comedy stage. Many hours were spent with my main contributor in comedy, Kelle. (This is her real name and, yes, she spells her name with an "e".)

I do realize that my stories carry a talking cadence. That is part of my writer's voice that is developing. In the Ponder Points, I found a freedom to do the extemporaneous writing that I do, instead of fighting those writing weaknesses I have: grammar, spelling, and focus. I opened the door and let them have freedom. Through this crazy fun, I find my stories. It has also given me a huge appreciation for my editors.

The editing for this particular book is different from the other books. I specifically asked that the edits be lightly done on the Ponder Points. This was to keep that authentic, far-from-perfect roughness that is part of the work. I am constantly working on my writing. I love it. There are mistakes. That is okay—another lesson I needed to learn as I embraced this lovely, messy writing life.

#47

MOVING FROM THE SURFACE OF THE SUN

This Ponder Point was written while sitting in the passenger seat as I had relinquished control of the car to Janine. It was a difficult afternoon for us both. Up until this day, I had been getting pages written for my novel. The working title was Frances. I do name all of my stories from the one-liners to the out-of-control eight-hundred-pagers. With Janine driving, I let my thoughts run away with concerns over the story I was not writing. I was basically sitting there in the car, a passive lump, not working on my unwieldly behemoth of a story. I was also stewing over the fact that I was not driving. Janine sometimes will remind me that she knew how to drive before we met. Plus, she had the really cool sports car and I drove a Volvo.

Because I was not driving, my mind was now spinning some sort of drivel about not being done with my book. That was not good as I found my thoughts drowning in doubts about my work.

Thoughts of being a failure before I even finished the novel were circulating and breeding with thoughts about practicing law in Fargo. Also, the sheer numbers of words and pages had me wondering why the novel was not done.

When we had pulled out of the corporate apartment parking lot three hours earlier. Dallas was still in our rearview mirror as we had made it twenty miles north to Plano, Texas. It was cook-an-egg-on-a-sidewalk kind of hot. Even though I had not written that day because I had spent it packing the car and cleaning out the apartment, I tried to be optimistic. By this time, I did have version number something completed. It was eight hundred pages long. I did not know it at the time, but I would basically throw this latest and most verbose eight-hundred-page draft out and start over. Most of it. I could have littered the highway from Dallas to Fargo with that draft. I did not because I don't litter, and I hope you don't litter either. The story gone, what was I thinking? I kept the characters. Well, some of the characters. And one character came to life in draft eighty-one and she is one awesome character. I'm so glad I did dump that draft because Molly Woods established herself.

It was reflecting on my writing while watching the miles of flat, dusty brown, sun-scorched fields pass that had me going through scenes in my mind. What worked in Frances? What didn't work? Man, this is going to be a long drive north. We chose Janine as the main driver to keep us from getting a speeding ticket. These flat open roads were just asking for fast speeds. At our current speed, we felt to me like a turtle crawling up the road.

My story sucks. How can I say it is done? I wrote it and can't tell you what is going on with it. How can I do this? Janine is depending on me. We spent a little over a year in Dallas, and I wrote something flatter than the road we were traveling with as much excitement as a tumbleweed stuck in a fence.

To stop the internal critic and machete-wielding editor, I decided to write. I pulled my computer out from the strategic location placed directly behind the driver's seat and started typing. I gave myself five minutes and no editing. My goal was to capture the humor in the stress of this day and find the flow of our latest adventure.

Hello All,

I spent the morning having a small packing breakdown, this being the first physical and mental breakdown I can remember having. Who packs a car in an oven? I did. Heck, I should have just taken a turkey and put it in a roasting pan in the garage while I packed so we would have fresh roasted turkey for the road. Our car was so full I could not wedge another item into the real-life SUV *Tetris* experiment. I could feel my tears of defeat starting to well up. Janine was at the office saying her good-byes and returning the company computer and her security badge. I'm glad she wasn't standing next to me with her linear brain helping. My bear was growling, and I am embarrassed to say that, as I type this, my grouchy bear is still mumbling.

On the floor of the garage sat ten odds and ends waiting to be packed in the car. My focus blurred. I looked from those items to the overly stuffed car and back. It was impossible. I had thrown my arms up and stared at the concrete radiating heat. It was over one hundred degrees Fahrenheit before noon and this was in the shade. Do I unpack and try again? Heck no. That is crazy talk. I retreated to the air-conditioned apartment and sat on the only chair available, the toilet.

Did we ever share with you that when we first met, Janine was moving to Australia? She said she would live anywhere in the world but would never live in Texas. It always fascinated me that she sent that to me in an email when we were working out the logistics of our relationship. I don't think we shared this with y'all because we didn't want to hurt anyone's feelings. What did I learn? Never say never because nine years after deciding we were exclusive—we moved to Texas. Our time with y'all turned us both into respecters of this country of Texas and of the people, the places, and the wonders that are there; however, I am still melting from the heat. I am not into the heat in Dallas.

Back to the packing of the car. I left the throne of the apartment and went back to the garage and the unpacked items, sweating like a horse that had finished running the Kentucky Derby. Just as I was ready to throw everything away, my phone rang. I saw that it was a number from the company Janine was working for and wondered if it was her. Would I tell her the truth about the packing breakdown?

"Hello?" I said with a quivering lip.

"Sheila. TJ here calling to say good-bye."

TJ, you did not know how you saved me this morning, and I need to let you know that right now. Plus, Janine is driving, and I am not sure how I feel about that right now, but we are going the speed limit. My first quivering words came out and TJ was over in minutes taking an early lunch. She, the daughter of an Army officer, had been drilled in the art of the move. TJ helped me shoehorn a couple more items into the car and graciously took a couple items that would not fit.

"Don't open those car doors until you arrive in Fargo," TJ ordered.

I hugged her and left quite the sweaty mark where my drenched arms touched her rather nice work clothes. I climbed into the driver's seat, pressed up against the dashboard, and followed TJ back to the office to collect Janine. There was barely room for both of us in this car. We said our final so-long-for-now and were on the road to Fargo. Exhausted, dehydrated, and hungry, I suggested that we stop for lunch before we officially got on the road.

Janine agreed, and we made it twenty miles north to Plano, Texas. Amy and Arlene had told us about a place that served bacon-wrapped jalapeno poppers. Kenny's was our first stop. The place was packed for lunch. We both laughed over the fact that we had not made it more than twenty minutes or so before stopping. People drive fast in Texas, and we stayed with the traffic so as not to get flattened.

As we enjoyed our meal of bacon-wrapped jalapeno poppers and excellent burgers, Janine looked guilty. She said that we had been invited out to lunch by the crew at work, but she used me as an excuse to get on the road. My response was to take a picture of us standing outside Kenny's. Don't be angry. I had sweated through my deodorant hours ago in the packing of the spring-loaded car.

TTFN, Sheila

#345

FURTHER TALES FROM THE DRIVE NORTH

Reading one's words out loud is a courage building experience. To help pass the time, Janine asked me to read my story, Frances, which was eventually retitled as Spectrum (but not until much later in the process and with great help from Kristen Tate). I pulled out my latest printed version, which took a ream and a half of paper. Yup, I killed some trees. She was still driving the speed limit even though we had not passed anyone else in this northern panhandle part of Texas.

As I started reading my words, my inner editor took out the largest chainsaw I have ever seen and went to work. I was crossing lines out and axing whole pages. Janine asked what I was doing. I told her I was reading the story. She had meant out loud. Oh yeah. Read your work out loud.

What does this have to do with the Ponder Point? I started to write again in order to not read my work out loud. Don't do that. Read the work out loud. It does help.

Howdy Y'all,

When one is driving on a freeway from Dallas to Fargo, it becomes an existential philosophical puzzle to measure progress in one's journey. The landscape does not change. Were we actually moving? Call it an attempt to keep our minds active or punch-drunk driving. No, we were not drunk from drinking.

The thought of going from the surface of the sun to the frozen tundra of the north had us both a little worried. To take our mind off the reality that we still only had minimal clothing appropriate for the below-freezing wind, ice, and snow that most likely covered Fargo in September, we talked about our fun in Texas. It did not take long before Janine and I were both in friend withdrawals.

These withdrawals are factually documented with many conversations discussing how much we enjoyed laughing, talking, and spending time with Texas folk. Also, we find ourselves cracking up over something we see on this journey, and we trip over one another as we both blurt out "oh my gosh 'they' would not believe this!" The ultimate form of compliment "they" defined: the horde of lesbians and great women brought together by TJ. I guess I could come up with a better name.... we want to call our 'curling team' the "Curling Beavers"! People who live in the frozen land of Fargo do curling as a sport.

Our drive north on I-35 on Friday had us laughing out loud because of two road signs set directly opposite one another. On the left side (of course) was a sign that advertised "Beaver Construction" and on the right side of the road was "Texas Women's University." That sort of funny just can't be scripted any better.

It took us a lot longer to get out of Texas than we thought it would and not because we were laughing so hard we were crying, and our abs were in pain from the increase in exercise from all the laughter.

I packed the car to a very critical point: the point when a packed car becomes spring loaded. Each opening of a door is done with held breath and a stance that might protect one's body from the flying shrapnel of crap that jammed our SUV to a possible breaking point. I might have repeated TJ's warning to not open the back and side doors of the car about every five minutes. The thought of letting Janine open a door without warning did not cross my mind. I want ours to be a long marriage. Plus, I really did not want to go through the packing process again.

As previously reported, we pulled out of the corporate lot at 11:00 a.m., but what I left out is that we headed straight to my doctor appointment.

Maybe it was the move. Maybe it was all the pressure that the work had put Janine through. But my heart was acting really strange. Good thing we went to the doctor. The fifteen-minute appointment took an hour due to the addition of having an EKG done.

Side note: It is important to be nice to the techs and nurses that help you out. Janine was sitting in the room with me and still can't believe I did what I did (really, and she has been with me for ten years). Just as Angie, the nurse tech, placed the next-to-last electrode lead to my body, I made a zapping noise and jumped. The result: Angie jumped back screaming and looked at her computer. Janine got after me through her giggles that I needed to behave and not scare the nurses and techs. Angie recovered enough to do the test. The EKG was fine. It showed my heart was throwing in an extra beat from the bottom of the heart every once in a while. I could find the down beat! This extra fun apparently is caused from lack of sleep, stress, and caffeine. Hmmm…don't know why that would be happening in our very settled life.

We also got our flu shots while in the office and boy that was fun.

Anyway, after the office visit we made it all the way to Plano before lunch at Kenny's Burger Joint, as previously reported. Now full of meat, we were ready to hit the road north. (Strange line coming from two former vegans.)

We drove another few minutes and arrived in Frisco, Texas where we stopped at GNC, based on a lead given to us by our doctor on meat sticks that have no added preservatives. It was now close to 3:00 in the afternoon and we had made it only thirty miles north. At this rate, we were scheduled to make it to Fargo in a week or two. Traffic on I-35 kept us in Texas for the next three hours. Oklahoma felt like it was a lifetime away from Dallas. Our music set to alternative female singers, we were going to be rolling on the road for years. Janine was still getting calls from the team she had just left. Work emails were still coming in too, and you all know that she was supporting those people who were reaching out.

I actually freaked out (but that is no surprise) over seeing a of couple state troopers and musing over the comedy of being stopped and having our protein powder in little plastic bags instead of the original huge-ass containers. Yes, I decided, I would consent to a search, but they would have to repack the damn thing when they were done. In other words, we drove the speed limit. By that I mean Janine drove, and I sat stewing in the passenger seat.

The drive allowed us both to reflect on our time together in Texas. The work. The people. The climate. Our conclusions: we fell in love with most of the people we met; the food is excellent (minus Tex-Mex); the climate sucks more than we could have ever anticipated; the shopping really is top notch.

Until later,
Sheila

#985

STILL ON THE ROAD NORTH

> *The art of telling the story and where to start was an issue with this particular Ponder Point. I wanted to capture the passage of time and work on the comedic elements of the little-noticed, mundane parts of moving. Like finding those comfort items one needs to feel human. Like wondering what the new adventure in Fargo was going to hold for us. Like the feeling of being trapped in a car in some of the flattest parts of this country. I surrendered to the feelings of being in the middle of nowhere both in life and in my writing.*

Hiya Folks,

Into the great unknown north, we drove with strange sounds coming from the spring-loaded car. Janine had wrapped up another panicked call from her old team wondering how they would survive the upcoming changes. It was then that we realized we were finally in Kansas. The sun had set hours ago, and we were both more tired than either wanted to admit. (No, we are not competitive or macho.) After years in the witness protection gypsy program, we look for places with comfortable beds. Hampton Inns make the mark when traveling through nowhere on an interstate. No Hampton Inn was located, and we were just seeing Bates-style motel after Bates-style motel. Finally, a Holiday Inn Express appeared, and we both let out a sigh of relief. Usually, I plan pretty well for the whole scamper and move routine. Like before, I had packed an overnight bag with all our essentials (toothbrushes, deodorant, clean panties, and lace).

Due to the packing of the car and the fact our load was indeed ready to burst at the slightest chance, we were not going to be retrieving the overnight bag. As it was, the blob of items kept pushing our front seats closer to the dashboard. Janine secured some toothbrushes and toothpaste from the front desk, and we both ran to the room and slept. Or attempted to sleep. It really looked like a set out of an Alfred Hitchcock movie. I woke at 4:00 a.m. unable to sleep. I was very good and did not wake Janine, although she must have felt my inner debate: Do I touch her or let her sleep? What would happen if I just tickled her with this feather that I pulled from the pillow . . .

For the next two hours, I debated better than Daniel Webster with the Devil. Apparently, talking to oneself wakes Janine up.

We were on the road by 7:30 after eating that yummy free breakfast at the Holiday Inn. The tables were filled with a group of seniors who were on a bus tour of some sort through the Bible Belt. We gave them something to stare at and wonder about. We were different. I guess they were jealous of my gold track suit. Breakfast for us that morning consisted of several hard-boiled eggs and a banana. Windows had to be unrolled a number of times for fresh air.

Because we both really only drink water these days, we have learned that restrooms are few and far between on the route we took north. Janine took over driving again under the guise that we did not want to get stopped for speeding. I crammed myself into the shotgun seat that was holding all the last-minute items. Not the most comfortable ride. At some point, I was held hostage because we happened to be on a stretch of road with no facilities. As hope was lost and I thought I might have to try and pee behind a rolling sage brush when a McDonald's sign appeared. Take exit 7. Relief was only four miles away. We saw exit 8 right after that sign and several miles later there was still no exit 7. I was stretching my abilities to hold "it" and about to lose "it." This was really the only time tense words were exchanged due to the fact Janine kept pointing out water along the road and trying to make me laugh. Yes. You read that correctly. Janine sometimes acts like a young adolescent boy with her jokes. Relief was finally found when we threw caution to the wind and took the next exit. It was not exit 7 but magically there was a McDonald's and nothing else.

The tension between us was finally starting to thaw and somewhere in Iowa we found a diner for lunch. Penny's Diner was filled with a bunch of women with bad haircuts and comfortable shoes. Most were sporting University of Iowa yellow and black. Janine and I felt more comfortable as we were not alone. Sappho lovers existed here in the middle of the corn fields. (Side note: The corn fields made me think of that horrid movie *Children of the Corn*—scary.) As we left, the 'sisters' (who just stared at us and never smiled) all of a sudden became Chatty Cathys. We said that, no, we were not going to the football game and we made our way into South Dakota.

Once we hit that South Dakota border, the roads got eerily empty. We went from a small traffic bubble to no traffic. I was looking for UFOs or some other explanation for the reason there were no cars on the road going north or south. I need to stop watching those end-of-the-world movies.

Legs crossed,
S.

#238
FURTHER TALES FROM NORTH DAKOTA

When I wrote this Ponder Point, I was working on a passage of dialogue in my novel, the passage that introduces the Buena Vista Cafe and how this becomes a central organizational point to the story. When I read written dialogue that flows, I am thankful to the author. It is a talent to write a conversation that feels so real you are in it. I wanted to accomplish that in my own writing. One way to capture dialogue in your work is to spend time listening to people and how they talk. It is something I learned with my dear friend Kelle when she and I dabbled in the land of stand-up comedy in Seattle. We would spend hours stealing characters and conversations from people at the Dog House (no longer in existence in Seattle) and other fun lounge lizard places. These next two Ponder Points are all about the conversations. I worked on capturing the magic that I was hearing.

Greetings Folks,

Life in Fargo, North Dakota, was settling into a new normal as our first week took on a surreal turn. The three- to five-year contract that had enticed Janine to move up to a place more remote than anything she had ever contemplated was possibly in flux. That stopped my search for a house to rent as we both decided to stay in the Residence Inn, with the fans of the University of North Dakota football team. The staff was most helpful and over the three months we were there, we did call it home. They gave us their kindness and wisdom about surviving the cold through the months of October, November, and December.

Midweek, our Mercedes SUV decided to act up. It might have decided that this frigid air was worse than living in the center of the sun in Dallas. Where was I going to find a place to fix this car here? I had seen plenty of Ford and Chevy trucks but not much in the way of the Mercedes being driven on the freezing roads of fall in Fargo. Janine had called from work and reminded me about the place across from the office building she was currently working in and that made me concerned on two points: 1) how could I forget because I had laughed over it; and 2) should we be scared?

It was the first Mercedes, Porsche, Audi, and Volkswagen dealership I have ever seen. Yup. All those car brands under one dealer. I did not have an appointment but decided to drive the car over there. Two minutes later I was in the service center. They were so nice.

"I don't have an appointment," I said to the young woman who came to greet me.

"We know that because our books are wide open with not a car on them for this time. What can we do for ya?" She bubbled over with helpfulness.

"Not sure what exactly is going on, but our car's electrical system seems to intermittently decide not to work, and it is rather disconcerting when driving to have the dash go out. Also, I was told to get a plug-in for the car? Not sure what that means," I had said.

"Well, I will have our guy look at it. You do need a heater for your oil if you want to start your car at all this winter. We can do that for ya too. Let me take you to our customer lounge, and I'll get back to ya when we know something."

I walked into a small and very comfortable customer waiting area. It was ten in the morning and the place was empty. I took my laptop out and was ready to work on the book when another customer came walking into the lounge from the garage area. I was trying not to listen to his conversation, but he had dialed his wife on his cell phone. He used the speaker function and sat the phone down on the counter by the coffee machine. This was the conversation, in a full Fargo accent:

"Hey honey, I'm drinking a fancy Keurig coffee and eating a complimentary Nature's Valley breakfast bar," the man said as he took another bite of the granola bar.

"What do you mean, you're drinking a fancy coffee? I thought you said you were going to save money for that thingy for the truck."

"Hon, they have a Keurig coffee maker in the lounge here, you don't have to pay. They have the pods here and the coffee maker empties that pod thingy on its own."

"No wonder that darn car the boys bought you is so expensive—they are spending money on fancy coffee machines. What is that you're eating? Why are you eating anything? I fed you breakfast right before you left."

By this time, I had to bite my cheek not to laugh because she sounded so perturbed about the car, the fancy coffee, and the fact he was eating something she had not made.

"Oh now, Nancy, don't be that way. The granola bar is complimentary too."

I had to get back to my characters, but the conversation continued on for a while and so I put on my headphones. I was comfortable and enjoying my own cup of fancy Keurig coffee.

A tap on my shoulder sent me into the stratosphere about an hour later as I was so focused on the world my characters were creating.

"So sorry, I didn't mean to sneak up and scare ya," she said, trying not to laugh.

"No worries. What's the verdict?" I asked. She took a seat in one of the black leather easy chairs that dotted the lounge.

"Come join me over here so we can have a chat."

"That sounds rather ominous." I was still trying to pull my heart out of my throat and sat down in a much more comfortable chair than the one I had chosen.

"I've got good news and bad news for ya. Which do you want to hear first? It doesn't really matter because I'm going to tell you both anyway." She giggled.

"The good news?" I said and tried not choke, knowing our car was out of warranty.

"The good news is the car is safe to drive and the guys know what's wrong with the car. We can install the oil heater for ya."

"What's the bad news?" I asked.

"We don't have the part. And the part with labor is going to be lots of pennies."

"Can you get the part and let me know exactly how many pennies?" I asked.

"I am a step ahead of you. The part will be here next Thursday, and I already have you scheduled. I put the report as to the costs in your car. I can walk you out to your car if you're ready? Plus, there is double good news. I checked, and the part actually will be covered under your warranty. You are so close, but it is still covered!" She stood, smiling, and walked toward the door.

I quickly gathered my items and wondered how things were going to work out in this land of freezing winds. As we were walking toward the car in their parking lot, she continued a rather friendly conversation. This is basically what the conversation consisted of and I shortened it to keep this Ponder Point reasonable.

"So, what's your husband do?" she asked, still smiling.

I had a mini discussion in my head. Do I lie? Do I tell her the truth?

"Well, I am married but I don't have a husband. My wife is here working for a group that is implementing a new software program."

She hit her hand against her thigh as she said, "I knew it. I can spot you people a mile away."

I wondered if that was because she was using a scope on a rifle. It was hunting season in this part of the world and everyone, including her, was sporting hunting camo wear. She must have seen my look of concern.

"Don't worry. There are lots of you people around Fargo. We have quite the arts scene. My cousin is a lesbian. Well, she is my cousin, but she was adopted. She's Korean. She went to the University of Montana in Missoula and told us she had met her wife and they moved to Portland, Oregon. Here's your car. See you next Thursday."

I sat for a moment in the car trying to get the feeling back in my fingers from the frigid winds. It was time to buy a pair of gloves. I pondered the conversation that had occurred and chalked it up to her being welcoming.

Ta Ta,
Sheila

#653
MORE FROM THE CAR LOUNGE IN FARGO

Good Morning,

Today finds me back in the lounge at the Mercedes, Audi, VW, Porsche dealership getting some TLC for our car in the form of a new part (thank god, it is covered under warranty) and getting an oil pan heater added. Yes. For those of you who live on the surface of the sun (all but our good friend Jean Bean, who lives in Boston, and Martha, who enjoys the beauty of San Diego), people must plug in their cars here in order to keep the oil from freezing. Janine was thinking that we could get away without doing this because she didn't see any plugs at our new home, the Marriott Residence Inn, but it turns out they have special plugs all around the exterior of the hotel just for the purpose of keeping those car engines warm.

Yesterday we met with the General Manager, Kim, and discussed our long-term stay with her. She brought along a most helpful sales associate (it was her first week on the job). Between the two of them, we learned where to get a great martini (one bar has Grey Goose vodka on tap, apparently) and that the oil fields in North Dakota are basically scary and not a place for two women to visit. I wish I had captured the look on their faces when I told them we spent the weekend in Minot for the Norsk Hostfest. (It was Scandimonium!!!!)

Janine asked about the oil pan heater, and the two of them both said that it pretty much is a must if you plan to drive your car in the winter. The sales rep then went on to add that there is no covered parking at the airport and she has come back late at night to find her car completely covered in snow. Yup. That confirmed the fact that we are going to try and find a garage to store our car while we are gone.

So today I am sitting in the lounge at the Mercedes, Audi, VW, Porsche dealership waiting on the repairs and the addition of the most attractive plug that will hang out of the front of our car. My idea was to work. It is quiet. My creative energy is at a strange high up here in the land of giants with funny accents. My quiet workspace was not to last.

The lounge now has two people discussing how to stay away from their respective grandchildren through the month of December this year. Why?

I can't type as fast as they are talking, but you are going to get the CliffsNotes version. Note: This is much funnier if read in the Fargo/Minnesota rolling accent don't ya know—yes, they really do talk that way here, and it's wicked funny (a shout-out to our friend in Boston).

GRAY-HAIRED LADY WEARING A SWEATSHIRT WITH PUFFY PUMPKINS ON IT (I THINK SHE MADE IT OR BOUGHT IT AT A CRAFT BAZAAR)

"Hey, Larry, I don't want to get sick like I did last year over the holidays."

BALD OLDER MAN WEARING A RED FLANNEL SHIRT AND BRIGHT ORANGE HUNTING HAT

"No kidding. It was awful, wasn't it? The whole family got it at our house."

LADY

"I won't say that I upchucked, but I did, and it was all clear. Plus, I had to play Santa's helper to Adam's kids on the 24th. I didn't dare eat anything and his wife had made prime rib. That was awful—she knew I was sick and that prime rib is my favorite."

LARRY

"No kidding. We all had awful body aches all the way up to the 24th. I told Hillary that we don't want to see the kids until Christmas Day this year."

LADY

"Great idea. Except I babysit the kids every Tuesday and Thursday, so Adam's wife can get some things done."

Lady never mentions her son's wife by name—is there some inner family drama? I so want to ask.

LARRY

"Guess that makes it hard. Could you just watch the kids through a window and not go into the same room?"

LADY
> "I wish. Those little kids are always hacking and coughing. It makes me sick just thinking about it."

I cut out another full discussion on upchucking. It was making me sick.

Later,
Sheila

#194

CONCERT IN MINOT, NORTH DAKOTA...ABSOLUTELY NO DANCING

Less than a month had passed since we moved to Fargo. My new favorite writing place turned out to be the lobby of the Marriott Residence. I was writing new scenes. Not that I wanted the page count to get back to eight hundred, but I was writing new scenes at a furious pace. One thing I wanted to work on was my descriptive voice. How well could I capture a place? The new scenes which would become a major part of the series were taking place in the Buena Vista Cafe in San Francisco. It was time to capture place. How do you do that? Use the senses—we have all five of them. If you need the list: sight, sound, smell, taste, and touch. Sounds easy to get those into a scene. I needed practice.

Well, Now... Hello All,

Janine, aware of my heritage, came home extremely excited from work tonight. For those of you who don't know, my heritage is Irish, Swedish, Dutch, Icelandic, and now I am repeating myself. At least, my parents think that is what makes up our family tree. No, I have not spit and asked one of those DNA companies to fill it in for me. Where is this heading? Janine and I are going to a Jennifer Nettles concert in Minot, North Dakota. She is the headliner Saturday night at Norsk Hostfest in the Great Hall of the Vikings.

"We're here in Fargo and she is playing in Minot. Why not go?" Janine said.

"Awesome. I'll get us a hotel room."

A couple things for those of you who are not familiar with North Dakota. Fargo and Minot are not close for a quick trip. They are 268.5 miles apart. Minot is part of the fracking business that was a financial boom for North Dakota.

"Our tickets get us into the Norsk Hostfest Scandimonium." Janine looked so happy.

We left on Saturday morning for the concert that night. I had looked up the distance after we had started driving because North Dakota kept going and going and going and going and going. The plan was to see Jennifer Nettles (lead singer from Sugarland for those of you who don't know) and then hit the Scandimonium festival on Sunday. After driving and driving and driving and driving and driving we finally arrived in a different world. The male to female ratio in this part of the world at that time was one woman for every three hundred men.

The grunge from the shale fields was everywhere, and there was a rather strong smell of oil in the air. Set against the muted color of dark brown covering quite a bit of Minot's surroundings, the flags of the Norsk countries were bright. We pulled into the parking lot of Norsk Hostfest as many people were leaving. I noticed as we walked in and were greeted by gnomes and trolls carved in wood that the festival was closing in forty-five minutes.

We literally ran through the festival, admiring the many sweaters as they were packing them up. I don't think Janine was disappointed the lutefisk stand was closed. They were sold out. No kidding. The other thing we learned as we ran through the closing vendor booths was the fact that this was the last day of the festival. It does not run on Sunday. What?! Who closes a festival down on Saturday? The upstanding, churchgoing folks of Minot.

We were excited to see Jennifer Nettles perform. I pointed out to Janine that we had lived in Dallas for about fourteen or so months and did not make it to a major concert. We had been in North Dakota for less than ten days, and we were going to Jennifer Nettles in Minot. She pondered that for a minute and then we found our seats. Janine is tall. She is also from the tall Northern European family tree.

I was short in this crowd. My parents saved all the height genes for my younger brother, Carlos, who is six feet four inches when he stands up straight. Carlos is not a Norsk name and that is a story for another time. The crowd around me was filled with tall, mostly blonde-haired people. They were a quiet group before the start of the concert. The Great Viking Hall had a couple thousand people in it, and it was like sitting in a library it was so quiet. Maybe they were all tired from the festival and Scandimonium celebrations.

Jennifer Nettles came out and did an amazing concert. Janine and I quickly learned that when in Minot, you do not dance or sing along. We were stared back into our seats and enjoyed the rock concert energy by keeping time with our tapping feet. What a stone-solid frozen group of people.

Standing still,
Sheila

#193

2 RUGBY, NORTH DAKOTA THE GEOGRAPHIC CENTER OF NORTH AMERICA, SORT OF...

Hi Folks, Don't Ya Know,

Our trip to Norsk Hostfest was not a complete bust. We got see Minot and what the fracking oil shale looks like on the people who are working it. They all were covered in a fine oil-like mist. Our drive back Sunday took us through Rugby, North Dakota.

I had no clue that Rugby is the geographic center of North America. They built a twenty-one-foot obelisk to mark the spot. There is not much around this marker, so it is quite easy to see. My curiosity got Janine to pull over, and I investigated this strange marker to find out that those town folks who claimed this geographic fact built a monument to celebrate it in 1932. We did the tourist thing and snapped pictures in the frigid cold.

Back in the car, I had to wait to consult Google on this fact as we had no cell phone coverage in this, the geographic center of North America. When we arrived back to our home in Fargo, the Residence Inn, I checked. It appears that Rugby really is not the geographic center. But they have a monument. The city has trademarked the fact, and you can get T-shirts and mugs. However, we were there on a Sunday. Not one store was open. Like their cousins in Minot, I suspect they were all in church.

Saying my prayers,
Sheila

#264

THE ELEPHANT IN THE WATER

One thing about my writing life that I noticed is that I work wherever we are, no matter what we might be up to doing. I work on vacations, on weekends, when at family events (I don't often let people know I'm working). I will capture quips, ideas, or scenes using whatever I might have with me. My phone is great. I snap pictures to help remember a place or situation. I use the record feature to capture quick thoughts when I am unable to type them in myself. I also have several programs for note taking and jump around from those that work on my iPhone or iPad. They keep improving, and I am hooked. I also usually have a notebook or journal of some kind within reach. If I am out without a notebook or my phone battery is anemic, I will write on napkins, scraps of paper, and books. Yes, I have even written on my own hand. Not the best because I have sweaty palms.

This situation was captured with a photo after it happened, and I wrote it down as soon as I was able to get to my computer. What I have learned through my nomadic life is to capture some aspect in a concrete form. There have been moments where I thought I would remember something because it was so fun, crazy, or strange only to have forgotten it. Now, whenever I hear a great name or something else that makes me pause, I write it down, take a picture, or preserve enough notes that I can recapture it when I desire. Even though I have a great memory, I make a very concentrated effort to record the situation. Life moves quickly through my brain even while on vacation.

In the Elephant in the Water I actually recited the events over and over again in order to try and capture the full effect. When I was dressed after our wonderful day in the spa, I wrote down the main points on a piece of paper I requested from the spa attendant.

Aloha All,

We are waking up here in Hawaii around 2:30 a.m. Monday through Friday because Janine is supporting those folks in Fargo, don't ya know. It is getting us used to working while it is dark outside. Fargo is rather far north and soon we will be working with Santa's helpers when the snows come. Because we are so far north that work will mostly be done in the dark as the daylight will be limited thanks to the tilting of the earth.

On with the Ponder Point for today:

Friday was an excellent day as we were given a day pass to the women's spa at the JW Marriott Ihilani. (Although it was mixed with the sad news that the hotel will be converted to a Four Seasons. I have been enjoying this spa for the past eleven years, so it is like family, and it was also part of the wooing when Janine and I first got together—a story for another time.)

Picture this: a softly lit women's spa with scenes of the beautiful ocean etched into fifteen-foot glass walls. A Roman hot tub surrounded by a tile mosaic, soft music, and no children allowed creates the serene backdrop to this Ponder Point about a possible faux pas. The spa, with its muted colors and healthy citrus- or cucumber-infused drinking water, plush towels, wafting scents of lavender and eucalyptus to soothe the soul, welcomed with peaceful serenity. A few women wandered in and out for massages or facials, but for the most part Janine and I had the run of the place for ourselves. We enjoyed the dry sauna, the wet sauna (reminded me of Texas in August, only it smelled better), the full body needle shower, the lap pool, pool-side lunch, and the Roman hot tub.

After an exhausting afternoon of floating in the lap pool (yes, I was thinking about my plot lines as I floated, so it was work), Janine and I retired to the private women's locker room to relax in the Roman hot tub. The jets were on for getting our tense muscles relaxed. Another woman, escaping her family, joined us and we were all quietly relaxing in silence. Iced towels rested across our eyes and ice water was refreshed by attendants; it was the most luxurious, restful setting, and we were being spoiled perfectly. The jets shut off, and I happened to be sitting directly in front of one of the air exhausts for the system.

Imagine the quiet, the silence, and it was all shattered as I was surrounded in a rush of noisy bubbles. It appeared that I had let a really big one rip. If I had, it would have been one for the record books. Janine shot up to a standing position, dropping her eye towel into the water. Her look of "Oh My GOD did you just fart?!" broadcast across her face. Because of her look, I immediately said, "It wasn't me! Honest...the system is just clearing out the air." By this time, the other woman in the Roman hot tub was now awake and looking at me too. Just then on the other side of the Roman hot tub (which was a good nine feet across by twelve feet wide) had another rush of bubbles. So, I said, "Look, I am a ventriloquist farter!"

Janine still gave me a look like I was the one who blasted the bubbles that rocked the Roman hot tub where I had been sitting. To prove this was not the case, we had to sit through another round of jets. As soon as they ended (I had moved to another spot in the vast hot tub) the water was very still around me, with not a bubble to be found. I pointed to my original lounging spot just as the enormous air bubbles occurred. I'm not sure why Janine still eyed me like I really had perfected the art of throwing my farts across the hot tub.

Relieved that I was cleared of producing my own Jacuzzi bubbles, I exited the Roman hot tub, put on my plush robe, and walked triumphantly to the ladies' restroom. I hung the robe on the hook supplied on the door. I used the facilities for what they were created for and flushed. Still triumphant from proving the fact that I did not fart in the hot tub, I was not paying attention to my plush robe as I put it back on in the restroom stall. As I walked out of the stall, I felt something cold and wet on the back of my right leg. Totally gross...I had apparently dipped my robe in the toilet water as I was so carefully putting it back on.

Until Later,
Relaxed Sheila

> *It was also at this time that I wrote the JW Marriott into my novel. For those who have read Spectrum, this was the hotel used in the scene between Frances and one of her love interests. I am sad to say the JW did close and many aspects that I loved about that*

property are now gone. It felt great to write about the hotel in Spectrum, preserving in my story.

#5
SALES, PERCENTS, AND MATH

This short story might confirm for some of you that I needed more time in basic math learned in second grade or third grade. On the writing side, I was working on pulling in multiple time points into a story line. In Spectrum, I was working on bolstering my characters: How much back story is needed to create a character and how do you introduce that into the story without ripping the reader out of the plot: I hate it when I am reading a great story and then the author's voice steps in and interrupts with something that doesn't make sense. I know that I am guilty of this in my own writing. This was an exercise to work two rather crazy retail experiences into the same time frame.

Aloha Fellow Shoppers,

Yesterday Janine and I ventured into the wild and wonderful world of Honolulu. One of our favorite stops hardwired into our shopping GPS (gay priority shopping) navigation is the Crazy Shirt Outlet store. This is a find of great importance due to the quality of their product. The sign in the window read "70% off entire store." Score big one for us because that meant the possibility of huge savings on some really plush T-shirts, sweatshirts, and other clothing accessories with fun, crazy sayings like "ski naked, ski fast." (This crazy shirt outlet is not just their Hawaii shirts—they dump all their regional shirts at the store.)

We found rock star parking and were walking into the store when the woman working on folding mountains of shirts said, "You picked the right time to come in because there is an additional 30 percent off." I took in that information and stopped in my tracks. 30 percent added to 70 percent equals 100 percent in my math world! Yeah, everything is free in the store!

Thank god, Janine and I are already married because this will make the second time in a store that I apparently lost my brain. The first time happened in a Home Depot when shopping for a refrigerator for an office space in Marin.

Tangent Home Depot story: The HD happens to be in Janine's top three GPS stores she actually enjoys. Not wanting to spend a lot of money on a fridge, we asked the woman wearing the orange apron if they had any specials on small fridges. She responded that they indeed had a couple options, but she wasn't sure if they were still on the floor. We followed her, and she led us to the perfect black fridge. It was larger than a dorm room fridge but smaller than one you would put in a kitchen. Not only that, it was deeply discounted. On the front of the fridge was a hand-written note that read "Slow Moving."

We got the 411 on the fridge and made sure it had not been previously sold and returned. It seemed to be in good working order, and the price was almost too good to be true. Before I go on, in my defense, I have not ever worked in retail. Concern crossed my mind and I asked the sales woman what the "slow moving" note meant on the fridge. Janine could not escape after my words were uttered.

To the sales woman's credit, she did not laugh. She did hesitate and wonder if I was really asking that question. Janine, through stifled laughter, said, "It means the fridge goes from zero to sixty in five minutes." Upon hearing her response, I realized that I had asked a really stupid question. The sales woman, still not laughing, said it meant the black fridge did not sell well.

Such is life for me. I put Janine in fits of laughter with my questions in stores, my strange logic in finding that 70 plus 30 equals 100 except when in a store and demonstrating that simple math is a skill that I make very creative. Every once in a while, I like to shock her with being able to pull out some fun and random math theory.

TTFN,
Sheila

#121
TURTLE ADDICTION

How does one write action? That is a great question and I work on it. Does the character walk, saunter, gallop, skip across the road? How do your people move in your writing? In this Ponder Point, Janine gave me the opportunity to work on action in a story. Hang on to your seats because this one has some action! Well, that was a big build up... Think about how people move through real life and then capture that in your writing.

Good Day to You All,

Yesterday, during our sunrise coffee break, we stopped to window shop along the way at the Marketplace, conveniently located along our path to get said coffee. The Marketplace is a brilliantly constructed trap for us wayward early morning wandering tourists. Bright lights, lots of color, and a huge number of overly cute stuffed sea creatures beckoning those soft-hearted individuals or small munchkins, or toddling biohazards known as children.

On this particular morning, Janine was lured to the window by the siren song of one overly adorable stuffed turtle. Our path took us right up to the window and a lengthy discussion on the cuteness factor of the various sharks, dolphins, stingrays, and turtles started. Now, I knew that my wife has a soft place in her heart for turtles. There was one snorkeling adventure on the Big Island where I thought I had lost her to the Big Blue as she followed a turtle out into the open ocean. (Yes, she did. It was all I could do to catch up to her and tap her fin to bring her back to the land of air breathers.)

In the years of being together, I realize that I will not lose Janine to another person; however, should a sea turtle woo Janine...I am done for and will have to concede.

I did not know I needed to watch her for signs of turtle addiction on land. As she moved her head and body to get better views of the wealth of stuffed tea turtles in the window, I hear a loud "WHACK." Yes. You guessed correctly. Janine had gone head first into the glass window pane, causing her great pain.

In shock, and stifling laughter until I knew she was still with us, I asked her if she was okay and exactly what she thought she was doing. She looked around, seeing some stars and birds floating around her noggin, and she said, "I now know what a bird feels like. I didn't see the glass window. I only saw the turtle."

I can attest that we had not done any sort of hallucinogenic drugs. Lack of sleep might be an issue; however, she also went onto explain, "Those turtles were just so cute . . ."

It is her addiction to turtles that caused her to ram her head into the glass.

Is there a support group for this?

Until Later,
S.

> *I am happy to report Janine did not suffer a concussion. I thank her for letting me include this story in the collection.*

#794
FART JARS, A GREAT GIFT FOR NEPHEWS

This is not so much a note about writing as it is a note of explanation. I have four nephews. They have grown into wonderful young men. Through watching these boys grow from little adorable blobs of baby into handsome men, I learned more than I ever wanted to know about farts. I have enough Ponder Points based on them to fill a volume dedicated to the Art of Farts. In Spectrum, there is a fart scene that takes place between Frances and a fart expert out on hike with his family. That fart expert is based on my wonderful nephew Ryan. He didn't think I could work his real-life story of breaking an exercise ball in his class and farting so loud it shook the walls into my novel. I did. You never know where your inspiration will come from and in what form. Thanks, Ryan, for sharing your stories with me and letting me work them into mine.

Happy Soon-to-Be-New-Year, Friends,

If a way existed to instantly teleport all our wonderful friends to join us bringing in the New Year, we would do it! Heck, I would have us celebrating around the world. All the top spots in amazing cities around the world. Okay, that would be a collection of wildest moments. Just imagine! For now, you all just need to know that we miss you and hope you are having a wonderful New Year's celebration filled with love, friendship, and laughter.

Side comment: How about that Notre Dame win over LSU? That was a quite the end to a wild game.

Like normal, Janine was up early supporting her client in North Dakota (thankful she doesn't have to travel to the land of 'don't ya knows'). For some reason, I was up at 3:00 a.m. Pacific Time and unable to sleep. What does one do when they can't sleep and are in bed with someone else who is sleeping? In my case, I wake them up to let them know I can't sleep. How well does this go over with the person who was sleeping? Must say it doesn't go over well at all, no matter how much they love you. Trust me, it is not a good move. Although Janine just kept repeating "sleepy time." Basically, if anyone was watching, I would look like a nut case because I was whispering in the dark. Finally, I just got my iPad out and hid under the covers taking over other people's towns/villages in my *Clash of Clans* game, not feeling guilty at all for probably stealing virtual gold from a six-year-old somewhere out there. I realize that I could have been expanding my brain; however, I learned that practicing a language in bed with someone trying to sleep also does not go over well either. Even if that language is the language of love.

Why not read a book? I like to read comedy and even though we are on an overpriced memory foam mattress, I can still shake the whole bed when I am in silent laughing mode. Note: Memory foam mattresses are rock hard if one leaves the window open and the ambient air temp is below freezing. Okay. I laugh a lot. The smallest thing can make me laugh. After spending a week with my two teenage nephews, I can honestly say that some of my DNA wiring is that of a teenage boy. When opening their gifts from Janine and I at Christmas, they did so with some trepidation. Ryan, age fourteen, asked if it was an empty jar filled with farts. (No, but what a funny gift. I will have to do that one. And no, I will not be filling the jar with real farts...the idea is enough.)

I wish I had captured the look on my mom's face when the fart jar comment was made. Apparently, she does not think that it is appropriate for someone of my age and background to be promoting fart jokes. Let me just say that for my birthday, Janine had given me a book on animal farts (with sounds). My dad saw the book and took it and silent laughed during the movie we were all watching. Gee, it is true the apple does not fall far from the tree. Unless the apple tree is on the top of a hill and the apple falls and then just keeps rolling down the hill. Then it could be far from the tree.

Later,
Sheila

Yes. Dad did play the fart sounds throughout the movie. I'm not sure if we were all laughing because of the comedy or my dad playing with the fart book. Sorry, Mom.

#47

PACIFIC NORTHWEST, BATS, AND FEAR

To catch you up on what was going on during this time, Janine's work ended in Fargo, North Dakota, quite a bit earlier than anticipated. She was in the midst of negotiating a contract with what would become her next client. That client was in Portland, Oregon. We were in limbo and were very fortunate to stay in the family condo in Sunriver, Oregon, during this lag holdover.

Sometimes I am amazed at how we transitioned so easily from Dallas to Fargo to Portland. I know it helped my writing through exposure to different people, places, and cultural specifics. At this time, I was reworking the background details of my characters. When the event happened, I used my writing exercise to pull together the past and the present. This idea was worked with more than once in Ponder Point writing exercises for me. In Spectrum, this concept of building the characters' pasts by including snippets in conversations with present friends helped the story develop in ways not anticipated.

Greetings People,

Janine and I are enjoying being back in the beauty of the high desert in Central Oregon. We are greatly missing our friends located everywhere but where we are currently residing (central Oregon). I wish I could convey to you all the beauty of the snow-covered Cascades, the Deschutes River in winter, and the deep blue of the sky. Yesterday evening we were privileged to see a great horned owl who took advantage of the street light that had just lit. In all his giant glory, he sat on top of the lamp post and waited until some small unsuspecting prey passed through the circle of light. In one quick, silent movement, the owl had dinner. Granted, that might be more information than anyone really wants to read about in the morning—after all I am not writing for *Mutual of Omaha's Wild Kingdom*. (Is that even on TV anymore?) Or maybe I am. Janine and I returned to the condo ready to call it a night after a day in the great outdoors.

Dinner done and the dishes in the dishwasher, it was time to call it a night. We were both grateful for the quiet nights of Sunriver. This is similar to camping only we are staying in a really nice condo with all the comforts of home. This has been a place that my family has vacationed in for over thirty years. Fun times at the condo. Except for this one time when I had come to Sunriver alone and had decided to sleep in the upstairs master bedroom because I could and no one else was there.

I can testify that nothing has ever woken me up screaming like having a winged animal first skim my face and then dive bomb me in bed. At first, I thought it was a bird. If you ever saw Alfred Hitchcock's *The Birds*, you would scream about that too.

When I finally fumbled with the lamp and got the light on and realized that what was frantically flying around the room was a very brown fuzzy bird, I screamed again. It was no bird: it was a BAT and not the kind you all use in softball. Yes. That is what happened. A small brown bat had somehow found itself living in our condo. It might have gotten inside when some work was being done and it found a nice high perch (the ceilings are eighteen to twenty-five feet in some parts of the condo).

Did I share that I was alone? What does one do when under the age of twenty something at two in the morning? I called my parents. They were not thrilled to be receiving a call from a daughter not in any real mortal danger at two a.m. Mountain Time. In Montana, they deal with everything from ants to grizzly bears, so my call about a brown bat was not earth shattering. A bat dive-bombing their oldest daughter barely registers. Their response was for me to shut the door to the room and go sleep in another bedroom. But first, they told me to go back in and open the sliding glass door so the bat could fly out. I put on a stocking hat, grabbed a broom, and ventured back into the bat-infested bedroom and followed said instructions. One bat inside is an infestation.

I did finally get to sleep in another room. The bat was never seen again, so I assume it took flight out the window. I thought about it flying out and getting all of its family and friends to come back and roost in the high rough rafters, but that did not happen. On that trip, the master bedroom door stayed shut and I slept downstairs. The family does continue to tease me about calling my parents over a bat.

Fast forward twenty-something years to last night. Janine and I are tucked in bed in the same master bedroom of the bat dive-bombings. Both of us are exhausted because one of us could not sleep and wrote from about 3:00 a.m. that day, and the other one supported her client (she was closing that account out) in the Fargo time zone, all of that followed by spending time in the fresh air and nature. Because sleep had eluded me lately, I had taken not just one, but two Advil PM's because I was determined to get a full night's sleep. The lights were off, and the wool blankets and comforter tucked all around to keep us toasty warm. The dark silence was interrupted by the sounds of something burrowing into a part of the room. We both heard it and simultaneously sat up in bed, listening.

"Did you hear that?" Janine asked.

"Yes. Don't move; let's see if it continues," I said. It moved again and was very loud. The sliding glass door was open a little to get the fresh cold mountain air. Neither of us moved as the sound of what I was sure was some sort of animal making a home could be heard. Secretly I was hoping it would be a squirrel rather than a skunk or raccoon. (I knew it wasn't a bat because they wait to dive-bomb you when you are asleep.)

"There it is again." Janine now pulled the covers up to her neck.

"Turn the light on," I said as I grabbed my phone and got up the courage to get out of bed and go over to the location of the noise. I checked the porch first to see if it was an animal outside, hoping it was and then we could just go back to sleep. No luck as the sounds continued. It was like a scratching, scurrying sound. It was unlike anything I could remember hearing. Mice you never hear; you just see their scat marking where they have been. It had to be a big animal because it was not stopping with the light and the talking.

I turned the flashlight function on the phone and started checking around the closet baseboards and around the chest of drawers where the sound really was coming from. I didn't see anything. No animal activity of poo or shredding anywhere. Still the sound. I concluded the animal must be in the wall, and so I knocked on the wall in various places and the sound stopped. Aha! I figured it out. There were no holes in the wall in the bedroom, and it was probably a big squirrel that had built a nest. (That was a hope because, somehow, they do not seem as yucky to me as a rat.) Raccoons are cute but scary smart and actually quite dangerous, so I really did not want to deal with that critter either.

With the sound stopped, I crossed the room and was getting ready to go back to bed, relieved that the animal wasn't inside the room. But the sound suddenly got louder. I went back, and this time determined it was coming from the chest of drawers. I carefully pulled each drawer open, peering in with my handy phone flashlight, ready to slam it shut should any eyes stare back at me. With each drawer pull, the sound continued but there were no alien eyes or any signs of an animal. But the sound was in the room, not in the wall. Because I do learn from previous experiences, I suggested that we just close the door and go sleep downstairs if we couldn't identify the source.

That was when I stood and heard the sound right by my ear. It is a rather tall chest of drawers. On top of the dresser was a plant, a carved wooden bear that had not come to life, and a partially drunk bottle of Perrier water. (You know I love my carbonated water.) The thought crossed my mind. No. It could not be the water. I picked up the now silent bottle and tested the cap. It was loose. I took the cap off. No pressure escaped the bottle, so Janine felt that probably was not the problem. I tried to recreate the noise, so I put the cap on tightly and shook the half-filled bottle and then undid the cap to different degrees of tightness. I never did recreate the noise, but it had stopped.

The critter had been a half-full bottle of Perrier water with a loose cap. Janine commented that it was good I had not approached the bottle with a baseball bat or broom. I downed the rest of the water and climbed back into bed. Sleep came after the adrenaline and burps from the carbonated water cleared my system. (Yes, I am such a lady...I can practically burp the alphabet—not really, but it would be cool.) The rest of the night was quiet.

Adios for now,
Sheila, the great hunter of Perrier Water

By this time, I had the full manuscript done that would become Spectrum. I had sent the manuscript to a couple of trusted friends to read. This was hard. I tried to use my time in Sunriver and our move to Portland as a distraction. It was helpful having these few special readers read what I had written. What I learned from that was to send a list of questions to help focus the readers. One person came back and told me the story would be so much better if I did not include the part about Frances exploring her sexuality. That I needed to give her a relationship with a man.

This sent me into a whole twisted inner dialogue, questioning my choices and how the story unfolded. Frances, my main character, had a strong talk with me. I followed Frances and wrote her story.

It is great to share your work with people you trust. Know that you will not please everyone and that is not your job. As I wrote the stories that made up the first two books in the F.O.K. series, I had to learn not to judge my own characters. That might sound odd because I am the one that created or captured them. There are characters I do not like in these stories. When I let go of judging my characters, the story opened up and become much better.

#29
GLAZED TODDLERS

How do we jump from the world of North Dakota to Oregon? Life is crazy like that and we did this jump in record speed. We were to be in Fargo for three to five years. That work did not pan out as the company was sold and the incoming CEO brought in his own people. Janine and I parked ourselves in Sunriver, Oregon as she hunted for her next gig. As you'll learn, we ended up in Portland, Oregon. By this stage I had actually whittled my story down from two hundred chapters to a more manageable one hundred and fifty, totaling six hundred pages.

To cut a scene, a character, an idea is painful. I would not know the full extent of this pain until I hired a professional editor. You are not alone when you have that scene you feel is so well written, so eloquent, and so right to be cut. I told each scene as I took it out of the Word document that it would be okay. I would save them in a special folder, and they would appear again. My desktop became littered with these tombstones of cut scenes. I have since organized them into a folder.

Be kind to yourself. However, you can manage to cut. Do it. This Ponder Point was one of the few where I actually practiced cutting as I wrote. It went against the original rules. For the first time, I wanted to capture the scene as a short story with a true beginning, middle, and end. It might have run over the five minutes but not by much.

Dear Friends,

In the search for a quaint, comfortable writing coffeehouse, I thought I found my mecca. Inspiration, for me, comes from everywhere. My search for the perfect ratio of electrical plugs to tables—mixed with a robust coffee and staffed by friendly people—was over when I found the Blue Kangaroo Roasting Company. The Blue Kangaroo is an unassuming looking coffeehouse nestled in the Sellwood neighborhood of our new hometown, Portland, Oregon.

The corner coffeehouse continues in the eclectic vein that so quickly falls into the cliché of Portland weird. A large, internally lit, sparkling pink flying pig with a blue tie watches over the coffeehouse from a most central spot hanging from the ceiling. Burnt orange walls show off this month's artist, a throwback to the colors and modular shapes of the 1970s. The paintings are filled with blues, yellow, browns, and orange. It works for this particular coffeehouse space. A couple well-used couches have lost the fight to push against the human that sits and instead welcomes the body deep into their cushions. If I didn't know any better, it almost appears that the furniture might actually swallow people up whole. To the right of the front door is an area created for the young two-legged humans. A pile of well-loved toys and a small blue table with four blue chairs on a sensory clashing bright orange, red, and pink carpet creates a romping and yelling section for children.

My schedule over the past week has been to deposit Janine safely at work around the 7:00 a.m.-ish time, give or take sixty minutes, and then drive south to the Blue Kangaroo. Upon entering the Blue Kangaroo, a friendly barista welcomes you and thanks you for joining them. It is a bit unusual but nice—not quite cult-like because this welcome is done before one orders any of the coffee drug or sweet treats dispensed from behind the counter. My eyes scan over the available tables. I note that five to seven others are busily typing away on computers or reading while they enjoy their coffee drinks of choice. I order and stake a claim on an empty table away from the children's section as I had made that mistake previously. It does not take long for this old pup to learn a new trick—like staying away from places where the biohazards, otherwise known as children, gather.

Monday morning all was serene. I had my yummy coffee. My characters were active and channeling their stories to me almost faster than I could type. But abruptly at 10:00 a.m., four other computer workers quickly packed up and exited the coffee shop. I glanced around, looking for a sign with a time limit, and saw none. A gentleman who was sitting in a chair reading a rather thick book was still deeply engrossed in the pages in front of him. No one behind the counter was chasing anyone away. But still, all of my fellow computer workers had packed up and run, almost like something scary had happened. I tuned back into my music. I was playing a Danish artist, Tina Dico, that morning and enjoying the ease at which the story poured out into words on the screen.

Around fifteen minutes later, I noticed through my peripheral vision that a couple of women pushing strollers had entered the Blue Kangaroo. Within another ten minutes, the place was filled with mommies with babies ranging in age from the ones that could fit in a baby carrier on mom's chest to the toddler set that is still in diapers but allowed to roam to a group of five under five-year-old somethings that took over the blue table and started coloring madly like little crazed artists. Why weren't they in school? Or maybe they were. Homeschooling is popular around here. Along with not vaccinating the little biohazards.

My brain registered but didn't bother to alert me to the danger I was in after the population of the Blue Kangaroo exponentially climbed in a matter of minutes. Out of the corner of my eye, I noticed a two-foot criminal with the distinct diaper waddle approach. I also failed to see that my bright turquoise headphone cord was dangling below the level of my chair and off the table. Somewhere I had some conscious thought that the little one had zeroed in on that cord. Based on previous experience, I figured the parental unit or monster caretaker would step in and herd him toward the kid zone or he would stop and just stare at the giant sitting at a table typing furiously fast, in total awe of the speed at which my fingers expertly pick out letters creating words.

Nope. The little walking munchkin grabbed the bright turquoise cord and pulled with the force of a superhuman toddler. It yanked the cord out of the computer and out of my headphones. Triumph filled the little blue eyes as he studied his newly acquired treasure. An avalanche of giggles shook his chubby cheeks, and it was at that moment I noticed this kid was covered in a glaze. Like a glazed donut, he was well snotted. I sucked down the gagging reflex as I registered that the mother of this walking snot-glazed little thief was mortified and apologizing. All the while the little tyke, named Tyler, would not let go of my cord. After some running, praying, and negotiation on the part of the mother, she succeeded in trading my cord for a juice box. The little terror sucked on that juice box much like I imagine a junkie sucking down heroin.

I held the now glazed turquoise cord with two fingers. The mother looked at me with a most quizzical look. I'm not sure why, as it was most acutely apparent to me that germs had been deposited on my now snot-glazed cord.

"Might I use one of those baby wipes in your bag to clean my cord?" I asked. At first, I thought the mother of Tyler was going to say something and then she collected her thoughts and responded by handing me a wipe.

I now understood why the other thoughtful computer workers had packed up so quickly and exited. Once my cord was clean, I packed up my computer, headphones, and characters and fled. A couple blocks down the street stood a Starbucks. I bit my lower lip and headed into the bowels of the over-roasted coffee place to sit and write. When my eyes adjusted through all the slick marketing and shiny happy people working, I recognized a couple of the computer workers from Blue Kangaroo. The clouds parted, and I understood the migration patterns of the Sellwood coffeehouse herds.

Safe from glazed children, I went back to work and was left pondering the reality of biohazards allowed to roam freely in public. A reported fact on Oregon Public Radio: parents will vaccinate their dogs and not their children. Ponder that one....

TTFN,
Sheila

#587
A BLENDED RAGE

Hey Everyone,

January in Portland is a lot easier than January in Fargo, North Dakota. The Curling Beavers never had a chance, but maybe we can start that team in Portland. Although they might confuse us as being part of Oregon State University athletic program. OSU's mascot is the beaver. The beaver is also on one side of the Oregon state flag. Oregon is the one state in the US that has a two-sided flag. Thank me when you get this at trivia night.

I was sitting in my car, stopped in traffic on a bridge in Portland. If you knew Portland you would shake your head and know exactly what I am talking about. On the local NPR station, they were discussing the cure-all for anything from skin rashes to obesity. What is this magic potion? It is the green smoothie. The green smoothie rage is everywhere. I sat back in the driver's seat and felt this rage rising up inside me. Traffic was stopped on the bridge because something was not working, and the bridge was currently halted in a half-open, half-closed position. Whatever ship had required the bridge to rise was long gone. People were starting to turn their car engines off as we were not moving anywhere quickly.

My years following a vegan/raw food diet flashed through my mind. The more the perky woman spoke about the magic of blended kale, the more my stomach started punching my brain.

"Don't you listen to that crap on the radio. You know it tastes like you are drinking your lawn. Of course, the moss-loving people of rain land would drink green smoothies. Let them...feed me meat," my stomach said, using my pancreas as a bullhorn.

I tried to get my stomach to calm down, but the rage was boiling. The woman was on the radio because she had lost six thousand pounds in one year consuming only gallons a day of green smoothies. She was handling calls from people expressing their interest, and I was screaming in my head but realized this was Portland and I should have just screamed out loud. The blending did not work for me and made me very sick. Weight issues have been with me since I started drinking breast milk as a newborn baby. I think breathing causes me to gain weight.

One thing I must point out about Portland that has not happened anywhere else: I was having a mental breakdown about kale smoothies stalled in traffic on a bridge. One would think I would end the torture and change the radio station or call a friend on my cell phone. That would be the logical thing to do.

Instead, I continued to listen to the righteous woman babble about how animal food is killing us all and that the only way to live was to drink the green smoothie. She based her findings on the fact that chimpanzees eat leaves. I'm still wondering how that correlated to a direct approval for drinking kale. I shut my eyes and continued to battle this woman in my head. I did not notice that the bridge was no longer broken. Or that traffic was flowing in the other direction. I stayed with my white-knuckled hands on the steering wheel, eyes slammed shut, wanting to find my own answer to my weight issues.

A knock on my window caused me to bolt my eyes open and jump up out of the driver's seat, hitting my head on the roof of the car. When I found my focus, I saw a man standing two feet from my window and pointing at the bridge. Behind me were about a hundred cars waiting to go across. I was now the knot in Portland traffic. I meekly rolled down my window and tried to recover.

"Hey, great NPR show. Do you think you can listen and drive?" he asked.

I mumbled a thank you and floored the gas pedal, causing the car to jump forward. Only in Portland is all I can say. No one honked. I would come to learn about the passive-aggressive character of this city.

Blender rager,
Sheila

#792
TO CONFESS OR NOT?

Greetings Ladies and Gentlemen,

Our second week in Portland, Oregon has found us staying in the way too swanky Pearl District. This is the remodeled, upscale industrial area of Portland's city center. Most of the really cool brick manufacturing or storage buildings are gone. A few dot the neighborhood, wearing new facades and sporting five hundred square feet of "loft" space for some pretty pennies. The spaces really are not "lofts," they are just small little apartments with concrete floors and exposed duct work and high ceilings. New glossy apartment and condo buildings make up the majority of the area now. Many have great views of the river and the bridges that make this a most interesting cityscape.

But I digress. Two nights ago, Janine and I were at a great little French restaurant on the edge of the swanky Pearl District. Le Happy is funky, not swank, and the food is excellently yummy. They specialize in crepes (savory and sweet) and killer cocktails. The tiny ten-table restaurant has stained concrete floors, deep red walls, and thousands of fake flowers stuffed in various places above the three-stool bar, down the skinny hallway leading to the restroom, and on the ceiling. Eyeglass frames cover a post and the rest of the wall space sports paintings from almost any genre one can think of from preschooler to Monet.

I think what I love the most about this dark little place, lit mostly by red light bulbs, is the gold door. The back of the front door is painted gold and it shines with a strange illumination. It looks magical, almost like you could walk through that door into the most amazing desires you can dream up. Although when we left the other night we walked out into the mist of a dark Portland street. In my mind I was thinking 49 Black Sand Beach, Big Island, Hawaii.

Back to the topic of this Ponder Point. Janine was wearing one of her great pinstriped suits, an awesome purple shirt with the coolest crystal buttons, and her cool shiny black leather dress shoes. I know she looked amazing and beautiful, and I am not just writing those words because I could be in some big trouble.

The waitress we had at Le Happy was handling a rather busy little restaurant. The three bar stools were occupied by some folks who must make this a ritual. They didn't need a menu for the ordering of their drinks or dinner. A family took over several of the two-seater tables, and we were able to secure one of the last empty tables pushed against a far wall and up against the coffee machine station. It worked. Our meal went at a leisurely pace as the waitress spent time talking with the three regulars on the bar stools. This was the same waitress who, when I walked through the front door, promptly shut the door on Janine. Not sure why, but she did. It was rather comical. I tried to stop the door from being shut on Janine, but that skinny woman was strong. Throughout the evening, I understood why she shut the door with such force. It was needed in order to close the gold door.

Dinner progressed as we were able to order. The food was worth the calories, and Janine and I were having a great conversation. Or at least the parts of the conversation I could hear were great. For some reason, I was having a hard time hearing Janine over the conversations that bounced off the concrete floor and walls of the little place. At one point, I thought Janine was talking about the outfit the waitress was wearing. This woman was wearing skin-tight black leggings and a black and white T-shirt that reminded me of a Parisian mime's outfit (and she could wear it because she was tall and a size zero and probably barely twenty-one). It was cute. So, when Janine finished her comment that I mostly heard (I clearly did not), I responded as I was watching the waitress attend to another table of diners, "Yeah, I think she's cute."

I realized something was up when the expression on Janine's face was one of confused horror. The waitress walked past, and the place did get a little quieter as the light bulb hit. Janine was talking about her suit—which she thinks is really masculine looking. In the ten years we have been together, I have referred to Janine in many flattering ways, but I don't think either of us recall me using the word "cute."

So, with the words "Yeah, I think she's cute" hanging in the air, I knew it was a moment of choice: To confess to your wife that you actually were not commenting on her but rather on a twenty-something young woman, or not to tell. However, Janine can read me quicker than a book. (I do not play poker with her; it is no challenge for her to beat the pants off me...did I say we play strip poker? Once.) I had less than a nanosecond to make a choice. This is what I did:

Me

"So you want to hear something funny?"

JANINE, LOOKING AT ME WITH NARROWED EYES

"Okay."

ME

"I realize that you and I were talking about two different outfits. You were talking about your pinstriped suit." My palms were starting to sweat, and I wasn't exactly sure how she was going to take this next part. "I was talking about the waitress's outfit." I had done it. I confessed.

Janine leaned back in her chair and started laughing. "Thank god because I would not refer to this suit or me as cute. Plus, you have never used the word 'cute' to describe me."

Ponder Point in this relationship is to always confess because Janine is going to figure it out anyway.

Typing from the closet in the dog house,
Sheila

With this Ponder Point I was working on capturing mood and comedy. Again, working with conversation and how to write the conversation. Spectrum was being edited daily and I was rewriting scenes and cutting more. I also wanted to work on tension. I was falling asleep reading my own story. How to infuse tension into a story? Real life gave me an example with this Ponder Point—a case of misunderstandings between two close people. It was after writing this that I realized I needed to add more than one love interest for my main character. It would be easy to give her the most perfect person after her horrid divorce. Life does not work that way. I had to kiss a lot of frogs that turned into trolls before meeting Janine.

#498

ADVENTURES AT THE FARM IN STUMPTOWN

When Janine and I happened into this Ponder Point, once again I thought I was done with Spectrum. The novel was re-written and self-edited down to five hundred pages. I cut scenes right and left. If it did not advance the story, I axed it. What happened after sweating my brain into deflation was the following. I needed an editor. I found one but not a good one. This was a friend of a friend who thought himself an editor. He basically smoked pot and talked about words. Not helpful. I was at a standstill with my book and my ideas of being a writer. I wrote this one in about twenty minutes. It is longer than most Ponder Points, but I was working on descriptions.

Dear People in Sunshine,

Last night, Janine took a break from work to enjoy dinner with me. My brain, in need of food, was not making any sort of choice around this concept of dinner. I felt like Tom Brady discovering that footballs have air in them and can be inflated or deflated. Directionless, I started driving in the direction of North Portland in the dark misty rain with no known destination in mind. Janine displayed a similar sort of brain paralysis from dealing with people in transition in the workplace. Oh, the set of characters she is meeting will indeed make it into a Ponder Point sometime in the future.

As the abundance of graffiti signaled that we had ventured into another area of Portland, Janine suggested a restaurant we had tried a couple years ago. It was a strange little coffee shop called Wives Tale. They specialized in a particular mushroom soup and tofu dishes. Food memory placed it in the file of rather good mushroom soup. It was almost 8:00 p.m., and Janine only had a two-hour break for dinner. I gladly took us out of graffiti-land and toward the known entity. Janine had looked it up to make sure it was open because Portland restaurants like to be closed on Mondays. Throws us back in time. Oh, the nerve of those liberals who believe giving themselves and their employees time off is more important than serving those of us who are not quite ready to cook on a hot plate or microwave in a hotel room!

In less than five minutes, I had us at the Wives Tale coffee shop only to discover that it was shut. White paper was up on the windows and the place was dark. Janine looks to her smartphone and says the website reported it was open. Then she looks closer and reads: "After thirty-something years we have closed our doors." They were closed and shuttered for good. Don't despair. We still had an hour and a half left before her next meeting. On our drive over to the now-closed Wives Tale, I noticed several other rather interesting food establishments that were open. Three of them were sushi bistros. Neither of us were up for raw fish.

"I saw a place called *Farm* with an open sign on 7th and Burnside. Let's try that," I said with a sense of adventure. Janine plugged it into her phone and saw that it had received some very good reviews. The saint of parking spots, Saint Mother of ALotta Space, smiled on us, and we were able to park on the street right in front of the converted Victorian house which was now a cozy restaurant. The neighborhood streets were busy with a mix of people. They ranged from those that were probably homeless to people in suits. Janine decided she needed to lug her heavy bag with computers into the restaurant. We fit the Portland crowd; I represented the dress-down aesthetic, in my comfortable shoes and a velour tracksuit, while Janine contrasted with her stunning Armani suit and shiny shoes. We were as odd a couple as ever did cross the rooster welcome mat and walk through the door.

We stepped into the hunger-inducing smells of rosemary, sage, and cinnamon. Soft lightening enhanced by oil lamps set in jam jars around the various windows and tables brought the red-gold tones out of the aged stained woods. A bright-eyed young woman sat us in the front window where we could watch the parade of people on Burnside. Janine and I were studying our menus when we both felt a light wispy presence approach the table. As if by instinct, we knew not to move too suddenly as we might scare her away. I was ready to relax and just be in the warmth of the Farm. Janine was still hopped up on work and thinking about the meeting she had later that night. Our energies caused the wisp to stand back about three feet as she first addressed us. Janine softened and that brought her closer, where she hovered near our table and, in an airy and uniquely comforting voice, introduced herself as our server. Before we spoke, she was gone. I started to laugh and look around for the cameras to see if they were filming an episode of *Portlandia*.

Janine asked me, "Was that real? Did you see that? Who did she remind you of when you first looked at her?"

"You mean other than your pocket person friend in Wisconsin?" (Janine has a friend from childhood is on the very tiny side of petite. In fact, her students on the first day of class thought she was a new student and not their teacher).

"Yes. Think cartoon character." Janine was now covering her face with her menu to hide the fact she was cracking up.

"If Olive Oyl and Pippi Longstocking had gotten together and had a baby—it would be this beautiful spritely creature who claims to be our waitress, but I am really not sure."

"Exactly!" Janine says.

Our dinner progressed, and it was wonderful. Then our waitress, who would float by the table at odd times, started to talk with us. She was a wealth of information about her transition to Portland from some place in Pennsylvania twelve years ago. Her first adjustment came in the grocery stores where people in Portland just like to linger in the store, blocking aisles with their carts. She said she quickly learned that you don't just push those out of the way here. It wasn't the east coast after all. Here, people are nice. Janine shared that we were new to the Portland area and this was our first time to Farm. The response from our waitress, again, had me looking for a film crew for *Portlandia*. This is what we learned, word for word mostly:

"Oh, well, hey, welcome to Portland—it is a great place. As I said, the people are nice here and they just like to stand and watch life and the wonder around them." (Note: she did not appear to be on any sort of drugs: her eyes were clear, and her skin was freakishly clear and smooth.) "Farm is a farm-to-table, sustainable, organic, locally sourced, seasonal food cafe in Portland. It is really great; we really love the abundance of the Pacific Northwest. Portland has so many great restaurants—it really is amazing."

I expected her to launch into the ancestry of the food we consumed that night, for instance to bring out a picture and biography of the lamb that went into the amazing winter stew I consumed. But she didn't. Instead she brought us a dessert menu and we splurged on the chocolate soufflé, which was velvety smooth and truly wonderful.

Later, our fairy waitress came back and took a seat to chat. We were getting used to her jumping and running every time a bell was rung. She would say, "Oh, I have to answer to the bell." And she would float away to deliver drinks or food to another table. Then she would float back to us. I really wish I could capture the sound of her voice. If I was casting for a wood sprite or fairy in the land of Narnia, I would want her voice.

She imparted her knowledge on the changing cityscape that is Stumptown. In Portland, before there were environmentalists and hippies, the loggers and capitalists chopped down all the trees, leaving stumps everywhere. I had always wondered about that nickname for the city of Portland. Flower, our waitress, shared that fact and many others with us. It was quickly approaching the bewitching hour for Janine to get back to work and attend a meeting at 10:00 p.m. I really didn't want our evening to end because I was fascinated with our newest adventure in Portland. Janine told me I had to stop studying and taking character notes on our waitress.

While this quiet wonderful conversation was happening inside the Farm, outside the farm we witnessed a drunk driver drive up onto the sidewalk. At least we think that person might have been altered in some way. A group of kids barely old enough to know any better picked up cigarette butts and tried to smoke them. A guy wearing a suit and not able to walk a straight line attempted to get into a car. Fortunately, he didn't appear to have any keys. Chances are it wasn't his car. Several people were traveling with their shopping carts filled with various items. Our waitress came over one last time and I commented on the diversity through the window. Her response: "Yeah. Strange, isn't it, for being such a central location to the city. When we first opened here there was nothing here. Now it is really cleaned up and almost classy."

On that note, we thanked her for her sharing and a most wonderful dinner. I got Janine back to work in time for her 10:00 p.m. call and went back to our home at the Portland Residence Inn in the Pearl District.

Night, Sheila

#85
BIKRAM YOGA, OR STAND AND SWEAT

In this Ponder Point I was working with the concept of cultural references. For the rewrite in Spectrum I decided I needed to put some cultural cues as to place and time for my main character. Some of the feedback I had received was the lack of knowing when the story was taking place. That helped. I wanted my work to be contemporary and to pay homage to those items that I enjoyed growing up. That was what went into this writing. References to movies, television characters, and capturing an accent.

Hi All,

The background that led up to how I found myself sweating from every pore of my body with about twenty other strangers started with Janine. Of course, she will say it always leads back to her and in this case it does. Sometime in our time together, the default for Janine is that I "blame" everything on her—The Good, The Bad, and The Unknown. This might be along the lines of the mysterious "we" pronoun that translated once married into "Janine" will do whatever task is awaiting. For example: 'We' need to fix the caulking in the shower. Allow me to translate: Janine fixed the caulking in the shower. 'We' need to bring more firewood into the condo. Translated: Janine schlepped firewood into the condo. It is like learning a new language. One that "we" are finding most entertaining.

Now on with the latest Ponder Point: As you remember, sweat was dripping from my body, creating a puddle of sweat so deep on my yoga mat that I could see my reflection. With each change in pose came another torrent of water. Basically, my skin was screaming at me because it is charged with keeping all the other organs at a comfortable temperature. I imagined a tiny little sweat gland engineer responding to the request for more sweat (use a Scottish accent here because this is based on *Star Trek*'s Scotty): "I don't know how much more she can take, Capt'n. I already have given her all we got. The last thing we have is some moisture in the bladder, but that would be nuclear stink, Capt'n."

Back to how we got to a room where I started to sweat pee because I was out of moisture. Janine met a very inspirational gentleman in Bend, Oregon by the name of Michael Harris. After meeting him in person and learning his story, we couldn't wait to try Bikram yoga. He suggested a studio in South East Portland. We met the women who run the studio and were excited to start. That was four weeks ago. Janine's work took hold, and she was drinking from the fire hydrant with twelve-plus hour days. We were not making it to the Bikram yoga studio anytime soon. Until this past Sunday. We were both committed to attending the 8:30 a.m. class. Nerves and apprehension infused both of us, so we were looking for the other to make it okay to push off such an endeavor for another rainy day. Only problem is that we are in Portland, and it rains every day. Shoot! I should know this type of weather because I lived in Seattle for several years (Go UW Huskies!).

We drove the twenty minutes south to the studio with mixed emotions of nervous excitement and curiosity. When we walked into the studio, the nice encouraging owners were not there. Behind the counter stood a sixty-something height-challenged man who was slight in build. His long gray hair was pulled back into a ponytail, showing off his Roman features and olive complexion. English not being his first language caught me by surprise. I had no clue what he was saying. He spoke a most interesting blend of Italian, yoga speaks, and English. Janine just smiled and nodded her head a lot. His voice was very lyrical and moderately deep, and so his sound captivated me for several reasons. First, had he been our first introduction to the studio, I probably would have run. Second, it turns out that as an instructor he was wonderful, funny, and very encouraging.

Our goal for this first time was to actually just stay in the room for the full ninety-minute session. Unsure of how my body would react to the heated room, set to 104 degrees and 30 percent humidity, "we" were clear on our only goal: do not bolt after the first few seconds. I took a spot right by the door. Several pretzel-like people were already in the room, stretching and meditating before the class started. They welcomed Janine and I and said that the first class is always brutal, and to hang in there and not run. With such recommendations, I shot a look to Janine that basically sent a thousand words as to why this was crazy, and we should just leave now.

Images of my one attempt at yoga in San Diego, CA several years earlier (twenty to be exact) flooded my mind. A friend, a yoga aficionado, talked me into joining her for a beginning yoga class. I walked into a room of people who were not beginners that day. Most appeared to have practiced yoga in the womb. I looked at my friend, Lisa, and shook my head. She said, "Don't worry, it will be fine." That day I almost died because (I really didn't know) the yoga instructor wanted me to do a tripod stand on my head. That is where you theoretically rest your knees on your elbows while standing on your head. I have been blessed by the boob fairy. I was not wearing the correct sports bra (for me, a straitjacket might keep them in place). On first attempt, I fell over into the person next to me. That woman was squashed—all sixty pounds of her. She was not amused and told me to go try and use the wall to help. It got me away from her. My friend, Lisa, was trying not to laugh out loud. I was. The yoga instructor came over to help me. She got me into the position and then I realized I couldn't breathe. My bodacious tatas had, with the help of gravity, basically cut off my air supply as they fell toward the ground. In desperation, I started laughing and fell out of the position choking, laughing, and crying. I was told that yoga was not for me. Not a very supportive group.

Fast forward to this past Sunday, where a short, older Italian man was saying "tis okay not 100 percent—you do 1 percent, get 100 percent benefit." Then he said some other words, but I have no clue what they were. He did have a nice smile and used the thumbs-up a lot. He told Janine and I to place our mats and towels in the back, so we could watch the other people in the class and learn. The others in there were very nice and quietly told us to just try and stay in the room. One woman said, "You might want to move closer to the door." I did. There was now a person between Janine and I, and I thought Janine was going to come put her mat on top of mine.

Everyone was facing in one direction, so I faced the other direction.

Then the little Italian stallion came in, dressed only in a European-style banana hammock. He said something to both of us. I just smiled and continued to nod. Then I watched others in the class and just tried to somewhat emulate what they were doing. It is a very different style of yoga. There are no hand stands. Thank god. The moves started with just some breathing exercises. What the crap? Since when did breathing become so difficult? Wait. My memory retrieved something—our time in Dallas, Texas. I got this! When I ventured outside in the heat of the Texas summer, it felt like someone had effectively taken all the oxygen out of the air. This 104-degree room with 30 percent humidity was easy compared to walking to your car in Texas.

Due to the fact they have no clocks in the room, and Janine and I had no knowledge of the movements, time stopped. My mind had no clue how long we were in there. A couple of times I caught my reflection in the puddle of sweat and thought, *what?!* Once my mind did wander to the question of time passage and how much time we had left. It was actually good that the instructor spoke in yoga Italian. I turned myself over to the journey in that room. Most of the time, I just stood and watched. I did attempt almost every move. There was a woman in front of me who was so darn flexible I had to watch myself and not stare open-jawed with the expression "You've got to be kidding me" clear on my face. At some point, my body seemed to lose the feeling of any pain.

The class progressed to floor movements. Thank god. Not only had we made it through the standing for over an hour, but also Janine and I had not run. I tried not to look at her too much through the class for fear we would enable one another to run. Actually, people in the class and the instructor encouraged us to hang in there and told us that we were doing great. I drank a lot of water while in that class.

Eventually the last pose was done, and the instructor encouraged people to stay in the room and work on poses. I stayed laying on my back, silently rejoicing in the fact that: 1) we had made it through the class; 2) no heart attack or heat stroke happened; 3) I actually was feeling remarkably clear-minded; and 4) Janine and I didn't run out of the class right after we both meditated for a few minutes. Granted, some of that was me wondering if I was going to faint trying to stand up again.

The results of that day were most interesting for both of us. Janine found that her mind felt really clear. I know my own mind was clearer and sweating like Niagara Falls might have something to do with that. I felt so sorry for the valet at the hotel when we arrived back after our class. Yes. We drove in our sweaty, pee stinky clothes back to the hotel to shower and change. I think Janine might have tipped him an extra dollar. That reminds me, I need to get a new air freshener for the car.

It was a great experience and we are going back.

Ta Ta For Now,
Sheila

> *A follow-up: we never went back. Our intentions were good; however, our excuses were stronger. To write is similar to taking care of one's health. Or not taking care of your health. I know I have writing habits that will make my editor scream. Thankfully, she catches most of them before you get the materials. Anyway, what I realized was I often thought I was doing a great job*

describing something and then I read what I wrote. My mind lied to the writer. It told the writer that she was doing great. You are getting all the details. Your words are flowing. They make sense. The reality? Nope.

From this Ponder Point on, I made sure to slow down. Five minutes is still a lot of time. With the inner critic/editor still off, I worked on pulling the descriptions out. On making sure that if I was working on active writing techniques, I still covered the five senses. What makes the writing relatable? I would jog through those questions quickly before I started writing. Seems like a lot, but I had made Ponder Points a writing habit.

#50

SIT AROUND OUR TABLE

How does a writer capture emotion? Convey the idea of love and friendship? I was presented with a writing topic that filled me with more emotion than I really knew how to control. This next Ponder Point was my attempt to capture a sincere and heartfelt rush of emotions.

Hi Everyone,

I found myself transported once again into a world of amazement and wonder. It did not start out that way. In fact, I started out rather grumpy. Just ask Janine. We had gone to bed the night before and the plan was that she would take her 7:30 a.m. call from the apartment. This meant I could sleep until 7:00 or a little later. I do not sleep well until about 5:00

in the morning. Janine claims this is a Sullivan family trait. I tend to agree; I think my parents, who never sleep, passed that gene onto me. You could call it a vampire gene; however, I faint at the sight of blood. This might make being a vampire a little difficult, and so I am pretty sure I am not a vampire. Or maybe I am and am rather anemic. My skin is so white it is blue. Thanks, Pacific Northwest. (Although Portland has had more sunny days than rainy days since we moved here six weeks ago.)

Anyway, that morning I was staring at my reflection in the mirror, wondering how in the world I get my bedhead hair. I was contemplating how everyone else in the world wakes up with perfect hair and mine looks like a group of wild birds nested in it, threw a party, and left the trash behind when they flew away in the morning. Through these random thoughts, I noticed Janine was fully dressed and applying makeup.

"Did the plan change?" I asked.

"Yes. I need to go into the office," she said, calm, cool, and awake.

"Do you want me to drive you?" I have a morning ritual and knew it was not going to happen. The stress was evident.

"I love it when you drive me. We can stop and get a scone and coffee at Finales on the way." She smiled as she applied her mascara.

I flew into overdrive and dressed quickly. I took care of my bedhead by throwing a hat on my head. The tangled mess of hair fought the hat, but my determination to hide the wild animal hairstyle won, and the hat stayed on my head. My ears were a little pushed out as I pulled the hat further down on my head. I was not completely awake, and my constitution was off. I growled a little as we rode the elevator down.

"When did you change the plan? A little more notice would be nice." Janine looked at me and smiled. Her smile disarms my grumpy attempts at growling (most of the time).

"In the shower," she said.

Through the drive on our way to the most amazing scones in the city of Portland, I started to thaw. It was better I took her to work so I could help get us settled into our new apartment. There were errands I needed to run. The scones were raspberry lemon and amazing. I hate to admit that the scone calmed my bearish brooding, and I was back to the smiling self I have worked so hard to bring back.

I got Janine to work and was on my way to pick up a couple items required for the chili and other errands that we all must do, when I got a text from our dear friend, TJ. It was the procrastination permission I was looking for that morning. I called. The conversation brought me face-to-face with the amazing workings of the human body again.

TJ's voice was a little softer, quieter than her normal self. I did not expect to hear the words "well, I had a little sort of a heart attack last week." Those words hit my brain like a crash-test dummy vaulting through a car window in a crash sequence. I stopped driving and pulled into the first parking space I saw. I sat and listened. As I listened, I realized how amazing it was that I was hearing TJ's voice on the other end of this digitized phone line. How her body, somehow survived the 99 percent blockage of a rather important artery. How her husband, Charlie, was now shopping for her like she was an army of rabbits. The fact that TJ was just chatting with us a couple weeks ago about life, work, and living in the flatlands of Texas.

As our conversation continued, I got this picture of how amazing the human body is and how much it wants to be healthy. I appreciated how insanely lucky I was to be hearing the account from TJ herself. It was sobering and scary and real, and it is life. With each word I realized how peculiar my internal reaction to TJ's news was because I was thinking about the beauty of the human body to heal. All these billions of cells we have that work together to make up the body we identify as "ourselves" really do want to be in balance and health.

My mind jumped around to the other miracle news I had witnessed over the past twelve months. One was my father's diagnosis of cancer and how his body responded to the chemo, to find life and humor again. His regained optimism has responded as a new life for him and those who know him. The strength of love shared between my parents is displayed by how they handle the unknowns, the fear, and my newest sibling, Chance, the Great Dane. Second was with a very close friend's diagnosis of cancer and fortunately a quick surgical solution. She joked that this was all much easier than having a C-section and a baby to care for afterward. Third was our friend who had a hip replaced after enduring a crazy number of years filled with hip pain. Before the surgery, she still actively played tennis, skied, and had the ability to grit through the pain. Now she is bionic, and I am worried I will not be able to keep up with her at all. The fourth example was talking to me on the phone and explaining how they took care of the blockage.

This morning, as the sun was coming up over the Cascade Mountain Range around 6:42 a.m., I wanted to set our kitchen table for breakfast. This breakfast would be a way for all of us to share, laugh, love, and enjoy the wonder that is life. In all these hard-to-hear medical issues are the most amazing stories of bodies that want to live. Bodies that will heal and allow us to continue to learn, live, and love along this path called life.

Around the kitchen table, we gather and share those things that delight us, those things that scare us, and those things that make us. The wealth of love, learning, and life that you all have given me is the most important treasure I possess. Janine and I have had the opportunity to move around this country, exploring life through people and places. This morning, I want all of you to join us at our kitchen table for a celebration of life.

The laughter will be infectious, the food divine, and the friendships timeless. Thank you, to each one of you, and I feel most fortunate enough to know you as my family and friends. We will always have a place set for you at our kitchen table. For me the kitchen table is the heart of the home. Stories are shared, food is shared, messes are made, and life continues. I appreciate the distances that separate us and so I challenge you all to share your kitchen tables. Don't care about the state of the house, or the hairstyle made by your pillow and a flock of wild birds, just enjoy the friends and family at your kitchen table.

Love,
Sheila

Update: We spent a wonderful morning in New York City in May 2018 with TJ and her family. They were there to support TJ's niece, who was singing at Carnegie Hall. TJ is doing great, as are the others mentioned in this writing. My dad is the only one who transitioned from this dimension we know as life. I had shared this particular Ponder Point with him before he died. We both cried together and he, the eternal optimist, said that he was fighting the multiple myeloma. Do not wait to let those you care about know how much you love them.

#2
THE TAO OF POO

Howdy Gang,

Janine has started her new job in Portland and is drinking from the "fire hose" in learning and meeting the new crew. One such meeting with an executive had her asking me if I had read the *Tao of Pooh* by Benjamin Hoff. Well, yes, I responded and went on to add that I have several copies of that book somewhere in storage. I used to give them to attorneys who annoyed the *'crap'* out of me. (Pun intended). "Why are you asking?" I was curious as to why the book was brought up.

She went on to explain that a man (of course it is a white male over the age of forty) asked her if she had read the book and then went on pontificate that he was just like the character Eeyore, the grey donkey, always worried about everything. When Janine shared this with me, my response was, "You have got to be kidding. Did he read the same book I did? Eeyore is not the character an executive, or anyone trying to lead a team, would want to tag themselves." More background:

The guy attended a two-week business course at Harvard and framed the certificate and had it hanging on his office wall. Insecure?

For those unfamiliar with the book, *The Tao of Pooh*, it is a wonderful quick introduction to Taoist principles as explained by the wonderful characters created by AA Milne. Eeyore is used to explain what negative, blocking energy or knowledge does to one's life. I will type slower so that point sinks in—Eeyore is used as an example of negative thinking and why one probably would want to limit that sort of behavior in one's life.

Janine wanted to get a copy of the book to refresh her memory. I wanted to get a copy to show her that this person has some screws loose.

We were in Sunriver this past weekend, and so Janine called the Barnes & Noble in Bend, Oregon to see if they had a copy. (She is going to pass the copy on to another consultant she is working with who has not read the book but was in the same meeting where this executive proudly called himself Eeyore.)

We had the title and the author's name and even the ISBN number. Janine called B&N and got a person on the phone. Now, it has been an assumption and probably not a well-deserved assumption that those who work at B&N are adept at looking up books by title, author, and ISBN number on their computers. I have been in line at said bookstore and heard people say, "I am looking for a book." The people are so polite most of the time as they tease out from the customer as many facts as they can about the book. All the while I am standing in line thinking, "No shit, Sherlock, you want a book...you are in a bookstore." They hem and haw because they don't know the title or the author but the story goes like this...then they basically give a plot line that makes me realize I am going to be stuck here forever. There are about twenty main plot lines that have been retold in millions of different ways since the invention of the printing press. Magically, though, the book fairy smiles upon the poor bloke manning the information booth at B&N and they come up with a suggested book and the customer says, "Ah yes, that is it!"

So, when Janine's call to B&N was going on double digit minutes, and she gave me a rather strange look, I wondered what was up. As I listened, she continued to try and coach the young woman on the other end of the phone.

This was their conversation, more or less:

JANINE

"I was wondering if you have a copy of *The Tao of Pooh* in stock? The book is by Benjamin Hoff."

B&N HELPER

"I have not heard of that—is that a children's book?"

JANINE

"No. it is a book on philosophy. Do you want the ISBN number?"

BN NON-HELPER

"I am not finding it. I did find *The Tao of Boo.*"

JANINE

"The title is *The Tao of Pooh,* it has been around for at least twenty years. It isn't really a children's book."

BN NON-HELPER

"Nope. I am not finding it."

JANINE

"I am on the B&N website right now, and it does say that your store has a copy. I just wanted to double check because sometimes the stock is not actually in the store."

B&N

"Really? Because I am not finding *The Tao of P-O-O.*"

Janine

"Oh no, not that poo. It is P-O-O-H as in the child's story *Winnie-the-Pooh,* but this is not a children's book—it is a philosophy book."

B&N

"I am so sorry. Yes. It does say we have one in stock. Do you want to come in and see if we have it?"

Janine

"The reason I am calling is to make sure you have it as coming to your store is out of our way, and before we make the drive, we want to make sure a copy is there."

B&N

"Do you want me to go check then?"

Janine

"Yes. That would be nice."

B&N

"Okay. I will be back." Insert stupid music..."Yes. We do have a copy and it is on the shelf."

Janine

"Could you pull the copy for Janine Brown and I will come in and get it."

I will stop the torture there because it took another few minutes for her to get the spelling of Janine's name. We did stop and get the book. But now I am inspired to write the *Tao of Poo.*

The book will be dedicated to the gang.

Rough sketch:

Tao is a philosophy credited as a Chinese principle that explains "the path" or "the way" through life, the universe and everything. Embrace the wonder that is life.

To be human is to poo. Basically, there is nothing more satisfying or metaphorical to life as good *POO.* It can be more satisfying then the best meal, best sex, best job. Or it could be painful and gut wrenching.

Stay Warm,
Sheila

#254

FOUR LEGS GOOD, TWO LEGS...NOT AS GOOD AND QUITE POSSIBLY A GENETIC DEFECT

Greetings Friends of J & S,

I know I have heisted a line from George Orwell's *Animal Farm*, but in this case, it works. There exists a new reality for the four Sullivan children who by genetic coding were all born with two legs. Our parental units will celebrate their fifty-second wedding anniversary this year. This is quite amazing and it is not lost on us that our dad has faced a different health reality. He has rediscovered his vigor and love for life. Mom and Dad continue to work on their dream house in the wilds of Montana.

The new reality is the fact that we have all been informed that we have a new sibling. Myths about fertile octogenarians in law school should have come with an asterisk and footnote. Before the arrival of our youngest brother, who is now eighteen months old, we would all hear respectively from our parents on mostly regular basis. Janine might mention here that the tether between parents and children was never cut—although, like in most families, that cord is stronger with the favorites. I am not a favorite, so I feel quite all right poking ironic fun at the family right now.

Mom and Dad would call and chat and check in with their children, who live in Hawaii, Colorado, Washington and, in the case of myself, it depends on the week. Currently, I am thriving in Oregon with my wife, which confuses my mother—a lot! To grow up in the Sullivan household was an experience, to say the least. The parental units, that we the two-legged Sullivan children chose, do not sleep. They demanded that we all be excellent students. Again, I excelled at one grade and that was kindergarten. Not to mention, they are a couple who truly believe in "use your time wisely and never say you are bored." Oh yes, and they are do-it-yourself people on steroids.

Case in point: They are in their early seventies and are chopping down their own trees, milling their own wood (yes, they bought a portable sawmill), and will build their own house (all 4,000 square feet of it!) in Montana. Granted, it was put on hold for a few months when Dad Sullivan was diagnosed with multiple myeloma; however, his chemo has given him back his energy and humor. The house building is on as they recently built their own septic system. The Silver Bow County Septic Tank inspector (how's that for a title?) told them the work they did was better than the pros who charge 40K to do such a large job. Pictures of the process were actually quite exceptional. It looked like the Keystone Pipeline for poo, built by Mom and Dad Sullivan, Chance the Great Dane, and one Bobcat.

Needless to say, for the most part we grew up participating in life and learning, thinking that it was normal for kids to come home and have to solve math problems for fun. Dad sometimes left us math problems on the whiteboard hanging on the wall in the kitchen. I wonder if my siblings remember that? Mom had us keeping our rooms shipshape and beds made with hospital corners. Dishes were never left. Chores were not allowance based. None of us were stupid enough to ever say we were bored with anything as the parents would quickly find some job that would whisk that boredom away.

Something though has happened to those same shipshape parents with the newest addition. Our little brother gets his undershirts warmed in the dryer before Mom puts them on him because it is cold in Montana. At Christmas, my older brother (nearing the age of fifty) and myself stood slack-jawed as we watched our newest sibling jump over the couch and run around like a wild crazed boy without a word of scolding from either parent. Instead, Mom and Dad celebrated how darn cute that maniacal run was because he was so happy his Daddy walked in the front door. When we were growing up, we were told that sofas were for sitting and not jumping over.

Who are these people and what have they done with our parents? When I was nine, I was practicing dribbling a basketball in the kitchen because the wood floor was similar to the wood floor of the basketball court. (That is my story and I am sticking to it.) Anyway, I may have hit the basketball a little hard as it bounced up and hit the light on the ceiling, knocking out one of the glass lamp shades. It shattered and broke. There was no trial. No chance to explain. I was in big trouble and the punishment was swift. I learned a lot about weeding the flower beds, polishing wood floors, and other required cleaning jobs.

The phone calls and texts from the parents are now few and far between. Last week, I wanted to call and have a brief chat with my mom concerning a matter of utmost importance to me. I prefaced the call with the concerns and before I could finish this is what Mom said: "I have to go—your brother needs to go for his walk. I will call you after." *Click.*

Okay, I thought. I will go get some things done and then discuss the issue later. The callback never came. Two of my siblings say they are much more relaxed because they no longer get the multiple phone calls from the folks. But they all noticed that the parents have gone in another direction with our newest sibling. To start is the fact they refer to him as our little brother. He is a dog, but not just any dog. He is now a Grand Champion Great Dane. My parents have fallen into the cult of the dog show world. We tried to do an intervention by showing them the movie *Best in Show*, directed by Christopher Guest. Mom was not amused and made several defensive statements throughout the movie.

I had to go get my own pictures of a dog show we went to see my parents participate in and every character in that movie was at the real-life dog show. It was uncanny! We documented the fact. My mother didn't like that either. This could be an example of why I am not one of the favorites. My mom claims it is because I had the words "Question Authority" stamped on my butt at birth.

Anyway, I am still waiting for the call. I texted my mom to see if she had forgotten. Nope. She is busy looking for a new sister for Chance, our newest brother.

Shrug,
Sheila

This Ponder Point came from a mixture of trying to find a background for my characters. Spectrum was now its eighty-something draft. Character development was important, and so I was working on that with this Ponder Point. In my mind, I was thinking about the writers and literary characters that I was sad to say good-bye to when I read the last sentence of the book. What made them so important to me?

Characters need multiple dimensions, and I was working on that in my writing as I continued to craft the story. This Ponder Point let me play with the present and the past. I am not sure my parents would agree with the theme of this Ponder Point. I did mention it to them.

Back to writing and this idea of character development. I am lucky. My characters talk, and they talk a lot. This gives me information about who they are and how they will react in situations.

#96
NIGHT OWL

My writing on the novel had stalled. I was stuck. Janine had read through the version I was now calling a complete draft. Still something was not working for me with the story. Actually, a lot was not working, but I would not know that until I hired a professional editor. When one works so closely with something for so long, it all starts to blur. I found myself rewriting the same scenes over and over. Stress of change was in our life once again.

Janine had been very sick, and we finally had some answers and solutions. I am very happy to share she is doing great now. I was working with a young woman who dearly wanted to be an editor, as well as with a close friend in San Diego on the manuscript of my novel. Both were able to give me some very insightful feedback.

The craft of writing is something I will work on for my whole life. Even though the writing with the book had stalled and I was stuck, I continued to write my Ponder Point exercises. I encourage anyone who wants writing in their life to exercise the writing muscle daily. Even it is putting down one sentence or less. Do it.

The small steps keep you moving forward even when you feel stuck.

Dear Friendly Humans,

This Ponder Point focuses on my quest for sleep. It occurred to me that my particular circadian rhythm is directly out of sync with Janine's circadian rhythm. Granted, she is a much better dancer than I because she easily finds the beat dancing with the music.

I, on the other foot, find the downbeat and throw everyone else off. It looks like I am in a fight with the music. This inability to match the beat rears its ugly head in crowds that feel the need to clap or do the wave. Next time we are in a crowd together, and everyone is clapping along to the music, I will be the one clapping in between everyone else. At this point in my life, I air clap. It is like being the kid in elementary band class who has not practiced, so they pretend to be playing their instrument. I have suffered—wait—I *enjoyed* going to my nephews' various band performances through elementary and middle school. They were excellent air trumpet players! Seriously, they knew how to play, and their school bands held the beat.

I did see a doctor, a professional in sleep medicine. Yes, there is such a discipline. During the past week, I followed her suggested sleeping schedule of 2:00 a.m. to bed and attempted 10:00 a.m. waking time. What does this mean? It means that Janine heads to bed like most people between 9:00 and 10:00 p.m. because she usually needs to be up at 6:00 a.m. Our sleep schedules are like trying to listen to classical music in the left ear and hip-hop in the right ear.

Last night, I attempted to make amends for this crazy schedule, which has resulted in us spending much less time together. I spent some time chatting with her until she fell asleep. The plan was that I would get up and get back to work, and Janine would get several hours of sleep before I came in to go to bed at 2:00 a.m.

Anyway, the room was dark, and Janine was breathing soundly in her sleep, so I tried to be quiet when I exited the room.

I went to retrieve my reading glasses from my nightstand and knocked over a glass of water. At the same time, I managed to hit the remote control for the bed. Yes. We have a remote control for the bed. Right now, I see images of driving a bed around like a remote-control car. It's not that kind of remote control bed. This remote allows us to raise and lower the head and foot of the bed. It is great because it has stopped my snoring.

Well, I hit the remote and sent both the head and foot of the bed into folding Janine up. She was being wrapped in a bed taco. So much for sleep as that woke her up. My knocking over the glass did not wake her but the bed trying to fold her in half did. Thank god she is so relaxed with me because she laughed and kicked me out of the room.

Fast-forward and it is 6:00 a.m. Janine had already risen and was out working. What she did was leave her phone behind in the room. This phone works as her alarm clock. It took me out of a nice snooze as the alarm sounded and continued until Janine came running back in the room to take care of it. For some reason, the phone was on my side of the bed. I rolled over and was able to get back to sleep for another twenty minutes.

I could hear her starting a conference call out in the other room. Sleep this morning was going to be a battle. That was when I started laughing because I had accidently tried to fold her in half last night. Not the thing to do to one's wife two weeks after she's had very extensive abdominal surgery.

Is my quest for sleep working? I am not sure because I am really tired right now.

Zzzzzz,
Sheila

THANK YOU

This first volume of the collected Ponder Points brought back the laughter and the points in time those short writing exercises were brought to life. Since I started writing Ponder Points, I have completed and published two novels and am working on the third. Ponder Points were my accidental writing lab. I still use the technique today.

It gave me feedback and direction in the writing craft that happened organically. Earlier, I pointed out that these small writing stints kindled my motivation to write. I exercised ideas and concepts in the writing without judgment. The larger part of this was sharing my writing with others and opening up to the feedback, both positive and negative.

To write is usually a very solitary process. It is for me. I like my time alone writing and often lose track of time. What I did not realize was how hard it was for me to share my writing with others. I hear you say, that is absurd! You are working on writing a novel. That means you want other people to read what you wrote. That is the romantic idea. You write a couple hundred pages and the story is done. Published. The world loves the book and you live happily ever after.

Yeah. Not the reality. I pushed off hiring a real professional group of people to work with me in the development of my work because that made it too real. If I continued to rewrite and edit the story I had been working on for years, it was easy. It was safe. Ponder Points helped me realize that people will read my words and enjoy them, share them, and sometimes not like them. Sometimes they will interpret what I wrote in a way I never intended. I have hurt others with my writing and that was not intentional. It hurts when a friend calls you on the phone and lets you know exactly what they think no matter how far it was from your intended meaning.

Through the years of writing that first novel, I did share it with a handful of close friends and my sister. They were wonderful, and I asked a lot from them. What I learned is that in order for me to move forward in my own writing craft, I needed to expand past the group of supportive people. I required myself to invest in writing. That meant the daily action of writing and the finding of professionals in the writing world. To be open to learning and taking the critical notes and learning from them.

My writing is so far a work in progress. That is what makes this field so exciting for me. Where is my curiosity and desire to constantly improve my skills in storytelling going to take me? I have met some wonderful people and some scary people—that glazed toddler comes to mind.

My hope is you enjoyed some of these words and hopefully some laughter. I do continue to write Ponder Points as they are my key to the writing day. I appreciate you spending time with these ponderings and would love to have you share your own Ponder Points with me.

Accidental Writing Lab Ponder Points on writing:

1. Write as often as you can. Daily is my routine. I am a writer and I write.

2. Read.
3. Ponder Points writing rules: five minutes of writing with no editing. Attempt to capture something that you experienced or is going on around you.
4. Find a great editor who can help you move your writing to levels you never thought you could.

TTFN,
Sheila

ACKNOWLEDGEMENTS

To my parents, Carlos and Sheila (Sr.), thank you for introducing me to the world of books at an early age. Yes, I am named after my mom. Thanks Dad, we all miss you daily. "Turtles all the way down and 42."

I do want to thank all those wonderful friends who did not charge me for new computer keyboards. You know who you are—Arlene, Amy, TJ.

A special thank you to Martha Shumaker, who adds elegance and love into our friendship and my writing.

Jean Choe, you are quick with your laughter and support. Thank you always.

Kristen Tate, you are better than a Maxwell Perkins! Thank you for your insights, your edits, and your kindness.

Thank you most of all to my wife, Janine. I love this adventure we are on together. Love you to infinity and beyond raised to infinity.

A THOUGHT ABOUT THE NUMBER INCLUDED

For those people who kept track of the actual number of Ponder Points in this first Accidental Writing Lab collection, yes, there are more than a baker's dozen plus two or a few more. There are twenty-one!

BOOKS BY
SHEILA M. SULLIVAN

Spectrum, Book One of the F.O.K. Series
Illumination, Book Two of the F.O.K. Series

Book Three Due out this Fall

Made in the USA
Middletown, DE
24 November 2020

25029669R00090